T.N.T.

TREASURE-HUNTERS 'N TRAINING

DESTINY IMAGE BOOKS BY KEVIN DEDMON

The Ultimate Treasure Hunt
Unlocking Heaven
The Risk Factor

T.N.T.

TREASURE-HUNTERS 'N TRAINING

EMPOWERED TO LIVE A DYNAMIC SUPERNATURAL LIFE

KEVIN DEDMON

DESTINY IMAGE® PUBLISHERS, INC.

P.O. Box 310, Shippensburg, PA 17257-0310

"Promoting Inspired Lives."

This book and all other Destiny Image, Revival Press, MercyPlace, Fresh Bread, Destiny Image Fiction, and Treasure House books are available at Christian bookstores and distributors worldwide.

For a U.S. bookstore nearest you, call 1-800-722-6774.

For more information on foreign distributors, call 717-532-3040.

Reach us on the Internet: www.destinyimage.com.

ISBN 13 TP: 978-0-7684-4119-2

ISBN 13 Ebook: 978-0-7684-8842-5

For Worldwide Distribution, Printed in the U.S.A.

1 2 3 4 5 6 7 8 / 16 15 14 13 12

Contents

Introduction

T.N.T.: Treasure-Hunters 'N Training is a guidebook for people who want to learn how to live a naturally supernatural lifestyle, expressing and demonstrating the Kingdom of God wherever they go, to whomever they meet. I have developed an easy, fun strategy to help you launch out in your supernatural destiny as a world changer and revivalist. I am going to help you become a treasure hunter. No, I'm not talking about searching for gold doubloons in sunken Spanish galleons.

By "treasure hunts" I am referring to an exciting model for witnessing that uses words of knowledge as clues to find people whom God wants to bring into His treasure chest—His Kingdom. Treasure hunting does not carry a "street witnessing" emphasis, which conjures up visions of preaching on a corner, arguing with people about theological nuances, or telling people how bad they are and that they should repent before God comes to strike them dead with His judgment. Rather, the goal is to find specific people whom the Holy Spirit has highlighted on the treasure map, people who need a divine encounter of His goodness and kindness expressed in signs and wonders, miracles, healing, and prophetic insights that call out the gold in them, which lets them know that God has good plans and purposes for them.

Treasure hunting has become the signature style of expanding God's Kingdom at Bethel Church in Redding, California, where my wife and I are on the pastoral staff. Furthermore, believers are now using the treasure-hunt model all over the world to find the lost treasures hiding in their families, friendship networks, neighborhoods, and communities.

As believers take risk to go find lost treasures, churches are springing up in Muslim countries, as well as many other parts of the world. I heard of missionaries in China who are using the treasure hunt to find child prostitutes. After being identified by the specific words of knowledge listed on the missionaries' treasure maps, these enslaved children find the confidence to go to the orphanage where they are loved and shown how to live in their God-given destiny.

We need a book like this one because most of us don't use the gifts of the Spirit as much as we could, and we tend to hold back from becoming too radical with our evangelistic efforts. Fellow treasure hunters help each other to ease past their natural reluctance so that they can be successful—even wildly successful—in their efforts to witness publicly to the reality of the love of Jesus Christ.

In addition to stirring up an initial willingness to step out of our comfort zones, the key component of treasure hunting is learning to use words of knowledge. The apostle Paul lists the "word of knowledge" gift in First Corinthians 12:7-10 as one of the gifts that the Holy Spirit gives to believers to help them spread God's Kingdom on earth:

> *But to each one is given the manifestation of the Spirit for the common good. For to one is given the word of wisdom through the Spirit, and to another the **word of knowledge** according to the same Spirit; to another faith by the same Spirit, and to another gifts of healing by the one Spirit, and to another the effecting of miracles, and to another prophecy, and to another the distinguishing of spirits, to another various kinds of tongues, and to another the interpretation of tongues* (1 Corinthians 12:7-10 NASB).

Words of knowledge might as well be called "clues of knowledge." Each one is like a puzzle piece or an indication that leads to more information—if we pay attention to them and can figure out what to do with them. When a team of treasure hunters collaborates with their word of knowledge clues, they can zero in on just the right treasures (i.e., individual people, most often unbelievers) whose hearts are primed and ready for an encounter with God.

As our words of knowledge provide the springboard to use other spiritual gifts such as prophecy and healing, God's love gets expressed in tangible ways to needy men, women, and children. When we step over the "chicken line" to take risk in sharing the Good News in practical, supernatural demonstrations, we often see what the apostle Paul explained when he made this observation:

> *If an unbeliever or an inquirer comes in while everyone is prophesying, they are convicted of sin and are brought under judgment by all, as the secrets of their hearts*

are laid bare. So they will fall down and worship God, exclaiming, "God is really among you!" (1 Corinthians 14:24-25).

The end result is that the Kingdom gets enlarged, as people recognize God's hand and realize how much He loves them. I have found that often as a result of this practical demonstration of God's love, people accept Jesus into their lives on the spot. Many of them are now treasure hunters themselves!

In the first section of this manual, which I have called Week One because I envision potential treasure hunters gathering weekly for a couple of months to discuss these eight topics, you can read the story of how I developed the treasure-hunt model. This method of supernatural evangelism soon led to my first book, *The Ultimate Treasure Hunt: Supernatural Evangelism through Supernatural Encounters*, which has encouraged Christians to supernaturally change the world around them.

I now lead supernatural lifestyle conferences internationally. I love to equip, empower, and activate Christians to learn how to take risks and step into their supernatural destiny. I also oversee a twelve-week Firestarters class at Bethel Church, where we train newcomers and new believers in a revival lifestyle—healing the sick, prophesying, and engaging in supernatural evangelism. As the director of Bethel Church's Firestorm ministry, I send teams of people to local churches for the purpose of imparting, empowering, and activating people in the Church to live naturally supernatural lives and to make it possible for the environment around them to be transformed.

Many people may never be able to come to Bethel Church or have an opportunity to spend time with us in person, and for them I decided to put together this manual, a practical book that models the treasure-hunting lifestyle. My goal is to equip and empower you to increase the impact you have within the spheres of influence God has placed you. To create it, I have pulled material from *The Ultimate Treasure Hunt* as well as from my other books, *Unlocking Heaven, The Risk Factor* (written with my son, Chad), and part of a compilation called *Hearing and Understanding the Voice of God*. Each one of these resources provides key pieces of information that, when combined, will ignite a dynamic, powerful, and explosive supernatural Christian life—T.N.T.!

Please don't read this book all by yourself just to learn the information I have presented. See if you can find someone else who may be interested in reading it with you or, best of all, a group of people. Although the concept of treasure hunting is exciting, stepping across the chicken line to do it can seem daunting at first. There is safety in numbers, however, even if it is just one other person. Working within a group setting will not only accelerate the learning curve, but also give you the courage to embrace the risk factor in stepping out in supernatural ways. Together, you can go over the thought-provoking discussion questions ("Let's Talk About It") that you will find strategically placed throughout the text of each of the eight sections in this book. In addition, most of the "activation" segments at the end of each section ("Let's Do It!") will require a team effort.

Your treasure-hunting team doesn't need to be massive—a handful of like-minded people will do—but unless you have the encouragement and example of fellow treasure hunters, you will most likely stop crossing the chicken line over time. Besides, what is more fun than playing a game with others? Of course you can and will sometimes reach out to needy people all by yourself, too, but you will not want to miss the enjoyment and encouragement that comes when you do it in the company of like-minded believers who are also pursuing a supernatural lifestyle.

In an effort to make the treasure-hunt model accessible to everyone, I have divided this book into eight parts that cover the eight most important aspects of what it takes to be a successful treasure hunter (a modern-day revivalist). After reading each section on your own, I hope that your group can meet once a week to talk about what you have read, and to launch out and give treasure hunting a try as soon as possible.

So after taking a look at the treasure-hunt model in Week One and risk in Week Two, I switch gears to talk about the vital importance of joy and laughter in Week Three. Then, in the fourth section of the book, I explore the foundational importance of knowing our identity as the beloved children of our heavenly Father. As you begin the second month of your treasure hunt training, in Week Five I discuss how to live a supernatural life of healing. Then, in the sixth and seventh weeks, I cover learning to hear His voice and how to receive words of knowledge and prophecy. Finally, on the eighth week, I invite you to take an in-depth look at our ultimate goal—supernatural evangelism—bringing people into the treasure chest, the Kingdom of God.

Throughout, I have tried to give you lots of practical and real-life examples of the topic of the week. My goal is to multiply the benefits of treasure hunting beyond what I can do by myself or with teams of people I have trained personally. To borrow Jesus' words from Luke 10:37, I want to equip you to "go and do likewise."

Each of these eight weekly sections closes with a prayer of impartation from me to you (by which I mean you personally and all of your friends with whom you are reading the book). Impartation is very real. It is one of those wonderful, supernatural ways in which a person can receive additional spiritual oomph—empowerment to go to the next level. I want to impart to you as much of the abundance I have received from Jesus as possible, so that my ceiling will become the floor or foundation of your breakthrough. I consider it my job as a leader in revival to equip you to be able to do "greater works" than I do.

As I mentioned, I have also interspersed the text with opportunities for group discussion ("Let's Talk About It"). And every week I have included some hands-on activity or activation ("Let's Do It!"), which I expect to be one of the best ways of activating that week's topic in your life.

You might want to split your weekly time into two parts: the first part for talking about the topic for that week, guided by "Let's Talk About It," and the second part for following through with the activation, putting legs under what you have just discussed. This will ensure that the material I have presented does not remain in the realm of the theoretical and that it gets reinforced in the best way possible, with firsthand experiences.

Here are some basic instructions on how to use this book as a group study. Before gathering, every member should read the chapter you will discuss. This ensures that the group time can be focused on discussing the material and answering questions, rather than on becoming familiar with the concepts. Next, discuss the "Let's Do It!" activation activities from the previous week. Allow everyone an equal opportunity to share, making sure that quieter members have time to describe their experiences as well. Celebrate and affirm each member for the risk he or she took. Next, encourage members to share their testimonies of risk from the previous week. This is an important step because sharing testimonies builds faith in us so we continue stepping out in risk. After hearing testimonies, discuss the "Let's Talk About It" questions from this week's chapter. Encourage everyone to share and take time to draw shy members into the conversation and answer questions about the material. Release the "Let's Receive It" prayer of impartation to the group and prophesy and heal each other as needed. Finally, read the "Let's Do It" section at the end of the chapter and lead the group in the activity. After the activation activity, take a few moments to debrief and discuss. Conclude by praying for each other. Remind group members to read the next chapter before the next class and to practice treasure hunting!

Throughout this manual I have tried to sprinkle many real-life examples from all kinds of "Ananiases." These stories are not just my own experiences. You will see that many of these stories describe healings, just as many of Jesus' stories in the New Testament do. By now at Bethel Church, and throughout the global Church, we have seen so many different kinds of healings that we have pretty much run out of categories for them.

Treasure hunting is never ever, boring. Our God is endlessly creative. Two of His many names are Healer and Redeemer. Father God obviously enjoys healing, redeeming, and restoring people to their complete destiny in His Kingdom, and He wants us to enjoy ourselves as we help Him fulfill His will for the world—making disciples of all nations.

In my first book, *The Ultimate Treasure Hunt,* I spent a lot more time talking about the "nuts and bolts," as well as key core values of treasure hunting. As you work through the *T.N.T.* manual, I would recommend that you get a copy of that book, too. I would also encourage you to find room on your bedside table for *The Risk Factor* and *Unlocking Heaven*, because they elaborate on the many principles and core values of becoming a fully empowered treasure hunter.

So, don't wait another day to become a treasure hunter. As you begin your training, my hope is that you would become empowered to step out of your comfort zone, to cross the chicken line, and to give it a try!

ONE

The Treasure Hunt:
The Making of a Modern-Day Revivalist

When my children were growing up, we would often play "hide and seek." There was an obvious thrill in their voices each time they pleaded with me to hide "just one more time!" and exhilaration in their eyes as they anticipated the surprise of finding me hidden out of sight in the closet or behind a door. "There you are, Daddy! I found you!" they would excitedly exclaim each time.

Of course, there would be no enjoyment to the game if I simply stood behind them as they counted to ten with their eyes closed. If I had done that, they would have found me in the first two seconds of the search. Conversely, if I hid myself so well that they could not find me, they would eventually give up and not want to play anymore. But because I wanted to be found, I would hide in such a way that they could find me when they searched.

I love what my friend and colleague Bill Johnson says: "God hides things for us, not from us." God, in His infinite wisdom, designed His Kingdom so that we would have to look for truth. He created us to enjoy the adventure of discovery. And yet some people have stopped searching for God, thinking He has hidden from them and does not want to be found.

The fact is: *Our heavenly Father wants to be found.* In Isaiah 55:6, we are encouraged to "seek the Lord while he may be found…." Jesus promised in Luke 11:9, "…Seek and you will find…." In James 4:8, we are reminded that if we come near to Him, He will come near to us. Similarly, when we seek to find the lost, we will find them. This study is meant to help you begin to find lost people supernaturally, leading to dynamic supernatural encounters.

I remember how I got started with the kind of seeking and finding that eventually emerged into what I call treasure hunting. When I first moved to Redding, California, at the beginning of the summer of 2002 to attend Bethel Church, I was putting in a swimming pool and I needed someone to help me dig a trench in order to bury the electrical wiring. It took several days to dig the trench, and on one of the days, I needed various items from the local hardware store. I took my digging partner, Chris, with me.

I soon found that Chris was not only an amazing trench digger, but also an amazing risk taker. At the hardware store, he approached person after person, asking if they needed healing for anything. He shared the love of God with them and prophesied about the good plans and purposes God had for them, sharing words of knowledge about the ailments in their bodies. Even those who had at first denied having anything wrong admitted that the words of knowledge were accurate. He ministered to about ten people over the course of thirty minutes, and a few were healed right there in the store!

Now, I had a lot of experience with street witnessing. I had even been on the Vineyard National Evangelistic Board. But I had never seen anyone do what Chris did that day— and it seemed so natural for him. I felt intimidated by his boldness, because I felt that I would never be able to take that kind of risk. (At that time, I even had to work myself up to ask people if they felt any better after I prayed for them to be healed at church.)

Over the next several weeks, I continually replayed what had happened at the hardware store. I knew that if Chris could do it, then I could, too. With some trepidation, I started reaching out to strangers in public by approaching people who had obvious ailments.

If I saw a man on crutches, I would step across my "chicken line" and ask if he would like me to pray for him, and then I would ask if he felt any different afterward. Each time, I could feel my heart nearly beating out of my chest, as the adrenaline raced through my body. Yet surprisingly, people started getting healed! Soon, I began to get words of knowledge for people regarding the ailments they were suffering from, and they would often get healed as I prayed for them.

This led directly to the treasure-hunt model, which utilizes words of knowledge to find the people God is setting up for divine appointments. I am confident that as you learn to discern His voice and take a risk to reach out to the people He highlights, He will also bring you to a higher level in your effectiveness at "spreading the fragrance of Christ" wherever you go (see 2 Cor. 2:14-15). As a treasure hunter, get ready to influence your family, friends, neighborhood, city, and whatever sphere of influence God places you in.

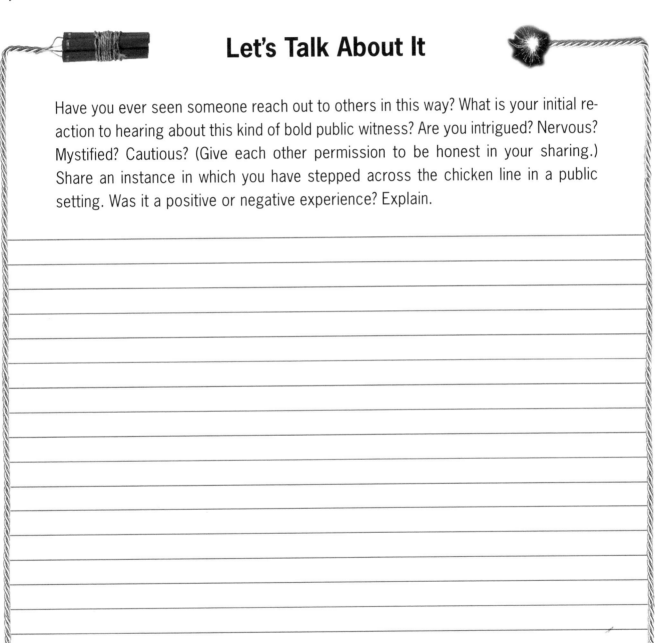

Let's Talk About It

Have you ever seen someone reach out to others in this way? What is your initial reaction to hearing about this kind of bold public witness? Are you intrigued? Nervous? Mystified? Cautious? (Give each other permission to be honest in your sharing.) Share an instance in which you have stepped across the chicken line in a public setting. Was it a positive or negative experience? Explain.

Working in Partnership with Jesus

Treasure hunts work in all kinds of situations. My son Chad took a group of junior high school kids out treasure hunting. After following several odd clues, they ended up in the parking lot of a well-known supermarket.

One of the kids had "a woman with a back injury" on his list. As Chad scanned across the parking lot, he saw a lot of cars, very few people—and an angel. That got his attention. Over a van in which a Middle Eastern woman sat, the angel was waving a banner that read "encounter."

Chad and his team approached the woman and asked if she wanted prayer. The woman adamantly declined, indicating that she was in a hurry. As the woman was backing out of the parking space, the "back injury" clue came to Chad's mind, and he yelled out, "You were in a car accident two weeks ago. You have pain in your back and it hurts to sit down." Absolutely shocked, she stopped in the middle of the parking lot and confessed that she had been in a severe car accident two weeks prior, leaving her with a debilitating back injury.

Then they began to explain to the woman that they were on a treasure hunt and that she was the treasure they were looking for. Chad explained about the angel that he had just seen over her van, and then he felt impressed to boldly tell her that Jesus had recently visited her in her dreams.

The woman began to cry. Through her tears, she explained she had been a very dedicated Muslim her whole life, but Jesus had recently visited her four times over the previous five nights in her dreams. She had not known what to make of the visitations. In the dreams, the messages she had received specifically told her to be expecting an "encounter."

Chad and the kids gathered around the Muslim woman and began to release the presence of Jesus on her. Immediately, all of the pain left her back, and she felt completely healed throughout her body. Chad talked to her about Jesus. Her response was earnest: "I want to know this Jesus that you know."

So there in the middle of the parking lot, this Muslim woman had an encounter that changed her theology in a moment. The team members did not need to argue with her about the differences between Islam and Christianity. Instead, they simply demonstrated the reality of the Kingdom of God in response to some "clues" they had received from the Holy Spirit, and they paid attention to the additional clue (the angel) that led them directly to a person whose treasured heart had been prepared to receive Jesus.

God Uses Ordinary People

Jesus has called every believer to live a naturally supernatural life. He has called each one of us to be a healer—to bring the Kingdom to earth so that what is in Heaven would be on the earth (see Matt. 6:9-10). Our mandate, then, is to represent Him on earth (see 2 Cor. 5:20). We are called to do what Jesus did, to demonstrate the Good News through a natural lifestyle of supernatural signs and wonders.

In Matthew 10:7-8, Jesus commanded all of His disciples to "proclaim this message: 'The kingdom of heaven has come near.' Heal the sick, raise the dead, cleanse those who have leprosy, drive out demons…." The command is still the same for us as it was for the first disciples. Each one of us, no matter how ordinary we may feel, is called to bring the Kingdom to earth in extraordinary ways.

Interestingly, Jesus did not look at John, the disciple of intimacy, and say, "Oh, I forgot, John; you are more of an introvert. I know that you much more prefer the 'secret place' of intimacy, where you can lay your head on My shoulder. I know that you are not an evangelist. Don't worry about going; I'll just send Peter. He's an extrovert. He'll say anything to anyone and take risk at every opportunity!" No, Jesus sent out all 12, regardless of personality, temperament, or gifting. He sent out the introvert with the extrovert, the timid with the bold, and the ungifted with the gifted, to preach and demonstrate the Good News.

In the same way, God has called each one of us to live an extraordinarily supernatural life. In my own journey of developing a supernatural lifestyle, I have always felt intimidated and inadequate when I have ventured into new realms of risk. I remain very conscious of my incompetence. I have also come to the conclusion that, if God can use me to do the extraordinary, then He can use anyone.

I do a lot of traveling to churches all over the world, equipping, imparting, and activating believers to live a naturally supernatural lifestyle. It is so much fun to watch people who have never seen someone healed (or have never even prayed for someone's healing) see a healing happen for the first time. Most of them say, "I can't believe that just happened through me!"

The key to living a naturally supernatural life is knowing that "ordinary" in the Kingdom is "extraordinary" on earth. This ordinary, extraordinary Kingdom is within us (see Luke 17:21). Therefore, it should be normal that, when we release the Kingdom of God through our lives, extraordinary things begin to happen—miracles, healings, prophetic insights, and deliverance.

God intends each believer to be a carrier of His extraordinary Kingdom, as the apostle Paul taught in Colossians 1:27, "…Christ [is] in you, the hope of glory." We are called to live a naturally supernatural life because "Jesus Christ is the same yesterday and today and forever" (Heb. 13:8). The Jesus of the Bible is alive in us today and wants to do the same kind of supernatural ministry through us. The Christ *in* us wants to escape *through* us so that everyone around us encounters His goodness and kindness, which leads to repentance.

Let's Talk About It

Talk with each other about what it means to live a naturally supernatural life. Speak from your own experience as much as possible. How many ways can you encourage each other to press into God for more?

Share an encounter in which God gave you some inside information about someone. What was the response? How did you feel afterwards?

What Is a Treasure Hunt?

Briefly, here's how we do a treasure hunt: A group of treasure hunters gets together before the group heads out. Each person writes down words of knowledge (the clues) to cover each of the following categories: (1) location, (2) a person's name, (3) a person's appearance, (4) what the person might need prayer for, and (5) something unusual.

After forming ourselves into groups of three or four, each of us keeps our own list, but we combine the clues to create our complete, virtual treasure map. Together, we choose a beginning location based on one of the clues from an individual's map, and we compare our other clues on the way to that location.

Once we arrive at our beginning location, we begin to look for the treasure, holding our folded maps in our hands. When we find someone who matches something that's on one of the maps, we approach the person and say something like, "This may seem a little odd, but we're on a treasure hunt and we think you're our treasure…." and then we show them the map. We get into a conversation and build rapport with this person. Sometimes more clues will emerge in the course of the conversation. We let the person know that God has highlighted him or her for a special blessing. We pay attention to the person's needs and we ask if we can pray for him or her.

If the person says, "No, thanks," we keep chatting to build more rapport while we also ask the Holy Spirit what He wants to show us about the person. We blend in words of encouragement (a form of prophecy) as we talk, avoiding religious language and pious behavior. Then we ask again if we can pray for the person. If the person still refuses, we bless that person and proceed to the next treasure (person). If the person agrees, we release God's presence and, especially if the need is for healing, we command the pain to leave, the bones to be set, and so forth, asking the person afterward to test out the healing by doing something that was impossible or too painful before.

After the person has been healed or blessed through prophetic words, we offer an explanation of what just happened by saying something along these lines: "This is God's kindness being revealed toward you. He knows you and cares about you." We go on to ask if the person would like to know Jesus and, if the answer is yes, we help the person ask Jesus into his or her life.

Oftentimes, I will ask people if they would like to encounter the Jesus who just healed them. If the response is a "yes," I'll ask the person to hold out his or her hands. I'll put my hands over theirs and instruct the person to simply say, "Come, Holy Spirit," or "Jesus, I want to encounter Your presence right now." I'll then ask the person to describe what's happening. It is amazing how many people actually feel God's presence in the form of heat or electricity, or as love, joy, and peace. I'll then invite the person to tell Jesus, "I want to encounter Your presence every day for the rest of my life." I explain the Good News of how Jesus came to sacrifice Himself on the cross so that we could have a relationship with God—the way they have just encountered His presence. And I explain how God wants to manifest Himself personally in all sorts of ways every day!

You can find detailed, practical specifics about treasure hunting at the end of this book in Treasure Hunt Resources I ("Creating and Using the Treasure Map") and Treasure Hunt Resources II ("How to Conduct a Divine Encounter: A Model for Healing Ministry"). You can find most of the same specifics in my first book, *The Ultimate Treasure Hunt*.

But what you just read is the basic way a treasure hunt works. The words of knowledge listed on our treasure maps enable us to find people who are precious to God, people He wants to reach. When a word of knowledge opens the door to witnessing, it creates an undeniable invitation into a divine encounter. God shows up as the all-loving Healer and Savior and people's preconceived notions fall away.

Why five specific categories of clues? While a treasure hunt can be launched from just a single category, I have found that having a lot of categories will help in opening up the treasure once it is found. Over time, I settled on these five basic categories as the most useful ones. For example, if we start talking to a woman in a hotel lobby because we have "hotel lobby" on the list, it is a lot more difficult to convince the woman that she is the sought-after treasure unless we can also come up with other specific clues, such as her name, the color of her clothing, a hidden ailment, or something unusual that nobody could have known without God's help. And when people see their clues already written down on our folded treasure maps, it is very difficult for them to deny that something unusual is taking place.

Let's Talk About It

Have you ever taken part in a treasure hunt or anything like it? If so, what was your experience like? Were you a treasure hunter—or were you perhaps the treasure? What did you learn (both helpful and corrective), not only about reaching out to strangers but also about yourself and about God?

_____

_____

_____

_____

_____

_____

The Ultimate Treasure Hunter

Remember the disciple named Ananias who came to visit Saul at a house on Straight Street in Damascus? In my view, Ananias was the ultimate treasure hunter. He was probably *not* a natural-born risk taker. He may have been introverted and untrained. After all, he was just praying at home when God spoke to him. He was not an apostle. He was not a deacon. He was not an evangelist. He was not even on the church "ministry team," as far as we know. And yet, as we read in Acts 9, in spite of his initial and fairly reasonable objections, God chose Ananias to lead Saul (who became the apostle Paul) to faith in Jesus. Look at how Ananias' experience lines up with treasure hunting:

In Damascus there was a disciple named Ananias. The Lord called to him in a vision, "Ananias!"

"Yes, Lord," he answered.

The Lord told him, "Go to the house of Judas on Straight Street [location] and ask for a man from Tarsus named Saul [name], for he is praying. In a vision he has seen a man named Ananias come and place his hands on him to restore his sight." [Prayer need.]

"Lord," Ananias answered, "I have heard many reports about this man and all the harm he has done to your holy people in Jerusalem. And he has come here with authority from the chief priests to arrest all who call on your name."

But the Lord said to Ananias, "Go! This man is my chosen instrument to proclaim my name to the Gentiles and their kings and to the people of Israel. [Prophetic insight.] I will show him how much he must suffer for my name."

Then Ananias went to the house and entered it. Placing his hands on Saul, he said, "Brother Saul, the Lord—Jesus, who appeared to you on the road as you were coming here—[word of knowledge] has sent me so that you may see again and be filled with the Holy Spirit." Immediately, something like scales fell from Saul's eyes, and he could see again. He got up and was baptized, and after taking some food, he regained his strength (Acts 9:10-19).

The results of Ananias' obedient response to the words God spoke to him continue to resonate even to the present day.

Having success in a treasure hunt depends on risk-taking obedience a lot more than on the ability to get all the right clues. There have been plenty of times I have found treasure with only one or two seemingly insignificant clues. Other times, I have found hidden treasure with no clues whatsoever, just as I was on my way to another location on my treasure map. And sometimes I have had several specific clues to identify a person as the treasure, only to be unable to find the person at all.

Treasure hunting reflects the culture of the Kingdom of God. All of us have had unpleasant experiences with pushy evangelists, just as we have also had such experiences with pushy salesmen. Treasure hunting is based on *service* ("What can I do for *you*?") rather than on greed ("What can you do for me?"). Too often it seems that evangelists are just interested in meeting some religious quota to find approval for themselves or to build church membership, rather than reaching out in genuine concern and love for people. The goal of treasure hunting is to broker an encounter of God's presence with the people we find. Jesus modeled true treasure hunting when He healed the sick, supernaturally fed them, and called out their destiny, thereby demonstrating God's love in ways that tangibly benefited them.

The culture around us demands, "You meet my needs," while the Kingdom culture says, "I will meet *your* needs." The culture of God's Kingdom is best summed up by these familiar words: "For God so loved the world that he gave his one and only Son, that whoever believes in him shall not perish but have eternal life" (John 3:16). God's motivation is not greed, but rather love. He sees us as His treasure, and He wants to bless us. The point of the treasure hunt is to convince people that they are God's treasure and that God is searching for them through us. Importantly, people do not care what we know until they know that we care, and they know that we care when we serve them the way Jesus served wherever He went.

We overcome people's objections by demonstrating God's love through practical acts of service that meet people right in the middle of their real needs. This is how the goodness and kindness of God can lead unbelievers to repentance (see Rom. 2:4). Often, after such a demonstration of supernatural love, all we have to do is pop the question.

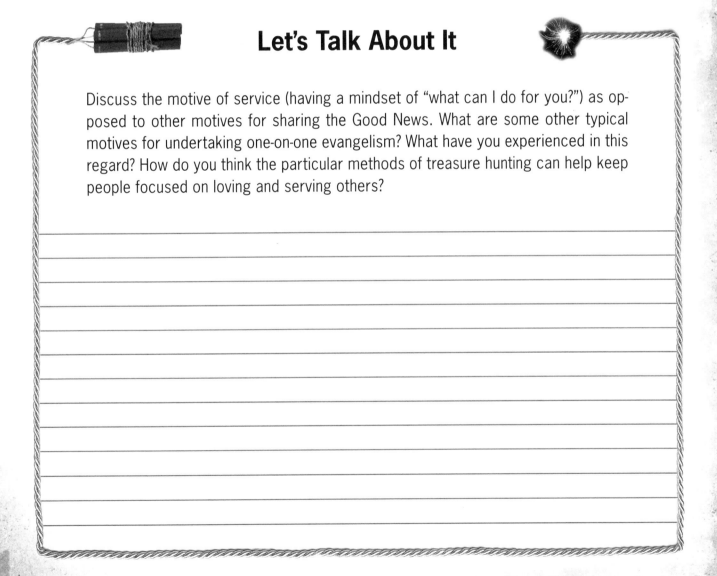

Let's Talk About It

Discuss the motive of service (having a mindset of "what can I do for you?") as opposed to other motives for sharing the Good News. What are some other typical motives for undertaking one-on-one evangelism? What have you experienced in this regard? How do you think the particular methods of treasure hunting can help keep people focused on loving and serving others?

Many years ago, I worked in high-end retail sales. I remember one new salesman who seemed to have a lot of potential when he was hired. He was great with people, immediately making connections and building rapport. He knew every detail of the product line and held the interest of the customer the entire time. He was a great communicator. His only problem, which turned out to be his downfall, was that he never asked for the order; he would never pop the question. Consequently, he hardly ever sold anything and eventually chose another career. I asked him about it one day, and he told me that he was afraid of rejection. That's the only reason he stopped short of his goal.

Getting Moving

Many of us have the same problem. We are anxious that people will say "no," as if that would hurt us somehow. We are risk-averse.

That's why I decided to devote the next section of this book to this very problem. Risk is one of the key words of treasure hunting, and we need to take a concentrated look at it so that we can step over our chicken line and into our supernatural destiny.

 ## Let's Receive It

I release you into your true destiny as a world changer and history maker, along with the confidence that you have what it takes to represent God and His supernatural Kingdom in whatever sphere of influence He has placed you. I declare surprising supernatural encounters during your quiet times, and daily activities in which God speaks to you and shows you specific ways to connect with the people He puts in your path. I pray that my ceiling would be your floor, and that you would begin to have your own testimonies of God's supernatural work through you!

Let's Do It!

1.) Fill out a treasure map. It should take about five minutes to get thirty clues. If it takes longer, you are probably working too hard. Remember, you have the mind of Christ, so your thoughts are the promptings of the Holy Spirit—write them down!

Then go on a treasure hunt with your group. You may want to do it as you go to lunch or coffee after your meeting. Select one person who seems to have the most confidence to lead out. Remember, when you find your treasure, make sure each person shows the treasure the clues they have on their treasure maps. Don't just tell them you have the clues; they must see them to believe them.

Go through the steps for a divine encounter with the treasure.

Go to the next treasure.

Afterward, debrief. How did the encounters go? How do you feel about taking a risk?

2.) Step out on your own one time during the next week to give someone a word of encouragement or to ask someone if you can pray for healing. Write down what happened and how you felt as you took a risk. Be prepared to share your experiences with the group when you meet next week.

TWO

Courage to Cross the Chicken Line: Revival Risk Renders Radical Revivalists

When we watch adventure films of skiers defying death on steep cliff faces or surfers atop sixty-foot mountainous waves that could kill them at any moment, most of us watch with envious admiration, thinking that we would love to have the courage to attempt such feats. Something inside of each one of us resonates with a desire for adventures and exploits.

As believers, God designed us to live by faith. The apostle Paul points out that "the righteous will live by faith" (Rom. 1:17; see also Gal. 3:11; Hab. 2:4). In other words, it is normal for Christians to pursue a lifestyle that is characterized by risk. You may not have the opportunity or the expertise to take on a sixty-foot wave or to ski down a double-black-diamond ski run, but at some point you will have to take some kind of risk in order to step into your supernatural destiny. In fact, without taking risk, there is no way to live *in* the faith and *by* faith. Without some kind of action, it is not faith at all. Risk-taking is the expression of faith.

The apostle James describes the correlation between faith and risk:

What good is it, my brothers and sisters, if a someone claims to have faith but has no deeds? Can such faith save them? Suppose a brother or sister is without clothes and daily food. If one of you says to them, "Go in peace; keep warm and well fed," but does nothing about their physical needs, what good is it? In the same way, faith by itself, if it is not accompanied by action, is dead.

But someone will say, "You have faith; I have deeds."

Show me your faith without deeds, and I will show you my faith by my deeds. You believe that there is one God. Good! Even the demons believe that—and shudder.

You foolish person, do you want evidence that faith without deeds is useless? Was not our ancestor Abraham considered righteous for what he did when he offered his son Isaac on the altar? You see that his faith and his actions were working together, and his faith was made complete by what he did. And the scripture was fulfilled that says, "Abraham believed God, and it was credited to him as righteousness," and he was called God's friend. You see that a person is considered righteous by what they do and not by faith alone.

In the same way, was not even Rahab the prostitute considered righteous for what she did when she gave lodging to the spies and sent them off in a different direction? As the body without the spirit is dead, so faith without deeds is dead (James 2:14-26).

Risk proves that we have faith. Without taking some kind of risk, we cannot say we are living in faith. God created us to undertake actions that involve risk in response to the level of faith that each of us possesses.

Living by faith is not a spectator sport. Instead of living vicariously through someone else's risk-taking venture, cheering them on from the safety of the sidelines or the comfort of the couch, each one of us must personally determine to step out and take action, in spite of our trepidations.

I heard of a high-wire acrobat who connected a cable between two high-rise buildings. A crowd formed a hundred feet below as the man took a few steps out onto the cable. The crowd gasped as he began to balance on one leg, and then twirled around and did a hand stand. Pulling a chair off the rooftop, he then miraculously balanced himself on one leg of a chair. The crowed erupted in a hail of explosive cheers, as the acrobat waved down at them with delight.

When the crowd finally quieted down, anticipating the next daring feat, he shouted down, "Who believes that I could walk across this cable stretching between these two buildings?" Confidently, they all shouted back that they believed in him. The acrobat responded back to the crowd, "OK, then, who will be the first to come up here and ride across on my back!" Not one of them took the challenge.

If we are going to step into our supernatural destiny, then at some point we are going to have to climb to a place beyond our comfort zone and be willing to live at uncomfortable heights of risk while balancing on seemingly flimsy foundations of faith.

Risk Is Entering the Danger Zone

Risk is defined as having the possibility of loss or injury. Risk is the potential of impending peril. We call it "risky" when someone or something creates or suggests a hazard.

We Christians are only living by faith when we are willing to walk the line, risking the potential of losing everything in the process. Jesus said, "Whoever finds their life will lose it, and whoever loses their life for my sake will find it" (Matt. 10:39). In other words, truly believing in Jesus means living a life of risk. And words are not enough. We cannot claim to be taking risk if there is no potential for some kind of loss or danger.

At some point, every believer must go beyond what he or she thinks is possible. You and I must be willing to lose our security, safety, status, reputation, and respect. In reality, if you are confident that you can accomplish something without the possibility that it might go badly, or not work out as you had planned, then you have not taken a risk. Risk only comes into play when we step out of the safety zone to enter into the realm of the seemingly impossible.

In other words, if we as Christians can accomplish something successfully on our own, then we cannot say that we have taken risk to do it. Our "job description" calls us to do the impossible. Jesus commanded us, "Heal the sick, raise the dead, cleanse those who have leprosy, drive out demons…" (Matt. 10:8). On your own, can you heal someone or raise a dead person back to life? Of course not. Only the supernatural power of God can provide the means to do that.

We have to start somewhere; we must simply step out. God is just waiting for you to step across your "chicken line," whether it's a little or a big expression of risk.

It definitely becomes easier to step out in faith when we can see other people doing the same thing. When we surround ourselves with risk takers, it becomes natural for us to become risk takers, too. Before long, we are promoting and propelling the culture of risk to others. I think that is why the writer to the Hebrews encourages us: "Remember your leaders, who spoke the word of God to you. Consider the outcome of their way of life and imitate their faith" (Heb. 13:7).

That is what Chris did for me that day in the hardware store. Watching Chris model risk gave me a vision of my potential in risk taking. I had never seen such a thing before. And being able to start small enabled me to attempt the adventure of taking risk in the supernatural realm.

Let's Talk About It

Where treasure hunting is concerned, where is your current "chicken line"? What can you do to cross it?

Risk Practice

I got my first pair of skis on Christmas day when I was ten years old. I was so excited. Immediately, I went outside with my new boots and skis to work on my balance as I stood in the snow on our front yard. In my mind, I pictured myself flying down a mountain.

My first adventure on the ski slope, however, was not flying down anything. Rather, I spent several days on the "bunny hill." I found that there was a big difference between standing in my front yard imagining myself skiing effortlessly and actually doing it! Once I conquered the bunny hill, I was ready for the rope tow, then the T-bar, then the chair lift, and then on to the bigger hills.

I will never forget the first time I attempted a black diamond expert run. I looked down the steep slope and cautiously began traversing back and forth, scared out of my mind. It was not long, however, until I simply aimed my skis down the mountain and took off with complete confidence as I accelerated to the brink of insanity in perfect stylistic form. Eventually, I got to the point where I could even ski "out of bounds" and jump off, and over, giant boulders.

How did I get to the point where I could ski so effortlessly while taking such extreme risk? I simply took gradual, increasing levels of risk, resulting in growing confidence as I conquered each new level of risk.

Similarly, each week in our Firestarters class we make our students take risks. Sometimes, without any prior notice, we ask them to prophesy to someone sitting next to them. At other times, we ask for volunteers to come to the front and we make them prophesy to someone whom we have picked out of the crowd. We do the same with words of knowledge for healing.

Amazingly, our "newbie" Firestarters always hear from God, even though, prior to stepping out in risk, they had never before heard a thing. There is something about being put on the spot that causes us to home in on His voice.

When we put ourselves in a position in which we *must* hear from God, we become more desperate and attentive. Pursuing a lifestyle of risk helps us develop spiritual hunger. If we never live on the edge, pursuing our destiny, then we feel little need to hear from God. Part of living a supernatural lifestyle is living on the edge of our comfort zone, because that's where our hunger for God's voice grows the most intense, and that's where we will be better able to catch the sound of it.

Let's Talk About It

Consider other types of risk beyond faith-risk, such as in my example of learning to ski, and talk about how you have grown as a result of taking increasingly challenging risks. Give some examples from your own life about taking various risks.

In our Firestarters class, we celebrate when people in the class step out into risk, whether it is giving a prophetic word to one of the other students at their table, giving a word of knowledge in front of the class, or praying for someone to be healed.

Each week, we ask the students to share testimonies of how they have taken risk to release the Kingdom throughout the week in their neighborhood, workplace, and school; among friends and family; and in the community at large. We constantly tell them that they have all of the gifts available to them, but that it is risk that allows the gifts to become evident. It is so exciting to hear testimonies of people who had never believed they were gifted until they stepped out in risk.

One week, a student shared that he was at someone's house doing a satellite installation when he noticed someone limping across the living room. He shared that the thought came into his mind that he had the ability to help out with the person's limp because he was a Firestarter. He went on to share that he "chickened out," doing nothing to release the Kingdom of God toward the person.

He sat down to the smattering of light, polite hand claps. Immediately, I stood up and told the class that we needed to *celebrate* his adventure into risk. "Think about it," I said. "Prior to this experience, he had never even thought about taking the risk of praying for a stranger for healing. This is an amazing breakthrough, and we need to celebrate his progress on his faith journey."

The next week, he shared that he was at another installation where someone had a physical ailment, and he actually stepped out in risk and asked the person to allow him to pray. He concluded that even though he had taken the risk, he did not see any breakthrough. This time, there was more clapping than when he had shared the previous week, but it was not at the level that it would have been if the person had been healed.

Once again, I encouraged the class to treat this testimony as if an incurable cancer had been healed. I explained that if we support people who are stepping out in faith to the same degree that we applaud a miraculous breakthrough, then we will eventually hear more testimonies about miracles, because more people will be encouraged to take risks. In response to the new level of understanding that they had received, the whole class stood to their feet, giving their fellow student a standing ovation.

The next week, the same man excitedly shared that he had met a woman who needed healing at another one of his installation sites, and as he took risk and prayed for her, she was completely healed! The class erupted in cheers. Not only had this one Firestarter student been activated in taking risk, resulting in a significant breakthrough, but the other students had also been encouraged to attempt risks as well, simply by observing the three-week journey of our supernatural satellite installer.

It is much easier to inspire people to take risk when they are in an environment that promotes and celebrates risk more than it celebrates success. Seeing the effects of risk taking in other people's lives makes us more apt to attempt what seems impossible.

Let's Talk About It

Celebrate the recent risk-taking experiences of your group members and each other's incremental progress as risk takers, whether or not they resulted in notable breakthroughs. Encourage each other in particular for seeming failures.

Getting Adjusted to a Whole New Lifestyle

Living a lifestyle of risk is like getting into a swimming pool. Some people choose to jump into the water without even testing the temperature, while others prefer to stick their toe in first to prepare them for what is to come. Some people just take the plunge, while others inch into the water. Either way works. The important consideration is that they are getting into the water.

Most people do not attempt risk because they think that only death-defying acts qualify as legitimate risks. Standing up in front of people to share a testimony may entail an *enormous* level of risk for some, while for others it is "easy peasy," and therefore would not qualify as risk for them. In a sense, then, risk is relative. What is risk to one person is not risk to another.

My wife, Theresa, oversees all of the prophetic arts in our School of Supernatural Ministry at Bethel Church. She is an amazing activator when it comes to teaching people to take risks creatively. She teaches that everyone has some level of creativity, but that many have been stifled because someone has told them or implied that they did not measure up to some hard-to-define creative standard. As a result, they stopped taking risk and therefore stopped growing.

Theresa constantly encourages her students to go to higher levels of extreme risk as they reach out to people through the creative arts in order to communicate God's heart to the people around them. She helps people go way beyond what they previously thought was possible, both in their own abilities and in the release of supernatural power through their artistic expressions.

As a result, we have seen many people healed as they simply held a painting. We have seen many healed when they saw a picture of a stick figure with a red X locating the part of their body needing healing. Amazingly, God uses any act of creative risk to release His Kingdom into people's lives.

One day, one of her students, Francesco, who happens to be an accomplished artist, decided to take a new level of risk in releasing the supernatural. He simply took a piece of chalk with him to the downtown Redding area looking for divine appointments. Seeing a man limping toward him, Francesco stooped down to the sidewalk and drew a simple square with the chalk.

As the man came upon the square on the sidewalk, Francesco asked why he was limping. The man explained that he had torn the ligaments in his knee and was in tremendous pain. Francesco, full of faith, promised that if the man would just step into the center of the square, God would heal him because there was a portal of God's presence in the square.

Skeptically, the man stepped into the center of the square. Francesco stepped back, watching as the presence of God instantly healed the man's knee! Francesco was then able to witness to the man about how Jesus had just touched his knee, and the man accepted Jesus right there in the square on the sidewalk!

So when did the portal of God's presence show up? Did Francesco see the portal and then draw a square around it? No, Francesco believed that if he drew the square on the sidewalk, God would come and fill it with His presence—and He did! That is how risk taking works in the Kingdom: God fills the squares of our efforts of risk with His presence and releases His supernatural power.

Jesus said, "Truly I tell you, if you have faith and do not doubt, not only can you do what was done to the fig tree, but also you can say to this mountain, 'Go, throw yourself into the sea,' and it will be done" (Matt. 21:21). The height of the mountainous levels of risk you are willing to take determine the level of breakthrough you will experience. Your mountain may be drawing a square on a sidewalk or trying to raise someone from the dead on the same public street. Whatever your chicken line is, believe that crossing it will lead you to the next level of breakthrough.

Pursue Risk

Risk taking is supposed to be a normal expression of the believer. In fact, it is this God-given capacity for taking risks that launches us into the impossible Kingdom purposes that He has prepared for us.

This Kingdom characteristic, however, is often underdeveloped and underutilized in the believer's life. Having been created with the capacity for risk, we must cultivate it as we would any other Kingdom characteristic such as love, joy, peace, forgiveness, encouragement, and so forth.

In Romans 12:2, the apostle Paul commanded us to be transformed, and he said that transformation takes place by the renewing of our minds. Likewise, in Ephesians 4:23-24, Paul encouraged us to "…put on the new self, created to be like God in true righteousness and holiness." In the Greek, Paul used the present tense in both of these verses for the verbs *renewing* and *being created*, which implies a continual action. In other words, we are to put ourselves into a position in which we are continually renewed, leading to transformation, because transformation is a process, not a one-time, all-inclusive event.

Thankfully, our growth and transformation are not completely dependent upon our own efforts—the Holy Spirit helps us in this process. In Ephesians 3:16, the apostle Paul prays that "he [God] may strengthen you with power through his Spirit in your inner being."

So then, we find ourselves in a partnership in this process of transformation. We are to continually *put on* what God is giving us, but His empowerment is what brings about any change that leads to transformation.

These principles apply to growing in faith as well. God gives us the grace to go to the next levels, but we must take the risk that releases us into the next levels of faith. I would like to wake up one morning and possess the levels of faith that I so admire in other people who take incredible risk to release the supernatural realm, but I know that I am going to have to partner with the grace that God has extended to me, as He invites me into my personal supernatural destiny. In order to do this, I must be committed to pushing the envelope of my current breakthrough.

We must *pursue* faith as a continual lifestyle. Risk will not chase us down—we must pursue it, looking for ongoing opportunities to seize the moment.

Let's Talk About It

As a group, discuss your own experiences of "pushing the envelope" where risk is concerned. Has it caused you to grow in faith? What has stifled your risk taking? What may be holding you back right now?

Taking Risks 'n Treasure Hunting

One time I was with a group in a Home Depot doing a treasure hunt. Among the many clues we had together, on my map I had written "red hair," "headache," Ralph," and "back problem." Walking along together, I noticed a woman with red hair about thrity feet away. I approached her and her husband, saying, "Hey, do you by any chance have a headache?"

"As a matter of fact, I do!" she responded. She explained to us that she had just mentioned to her husband that she was going to have to leave their full cart because she had developed a severe migraine since coming into the store about an hour before that. She was absolutely shocked that I had some inside information that no one except her husband could have known.

After explaining that God speaks to us and that He had clearly highlighted her, I asked if we could pray for her. She heartily agreed, while her husband, who stood 6 feet 4 inches and weighed about 250 pounds, took a few steps back to quietly observe.

In a matter of seconds, the woman reported that she felt heat on the back of her head where I had placed my hand to pray for her. Immediately, her headache vanished and she started to cry, overwhelmed that God would care enough about her to send us to help her. Even though she was not a Christian, she gladly let us pray for her again, and then asked Jesus into her life right there in the middle of Home Depot. Mission accomplished.

But then as we were walking away, I realized that I also had the name "Ralph" on my treasure map. From about twenty feet away, I yelled back to the husband of the woman who had just been healed, "Hey, I forgot to ask, but by any chance is your name Ralph?"

"As a matter of fact, it is," he responded. At that, we went back to show him the treasure map on which his name was located.

Now Ralph had been standing off to the side the entire time we were ministering to his wife. He had appeared very skeptical and was unresponsive to anything that had happened to his wife. But this word of knowledge (the fact that we knew his name) piqued his interest. I began to go down the various clues on our treasure maps, and at each ailment, he matter-of-factly denied having them. When I got to "back problem," he did the same, but this time his wife spoke up and said, "Come on, Ralph; you know you cannot even reach down and touch your feet because your back hurts so bad."

It turned out that Ralph had suffered a work injury that had forced him onto disability. I explained that God could heal him in the same way that He had just healed his wife, but he declined, saying, "Oh, no. That's OK; I'll be all right."

His wife immediately chimed in with, "Come on, Ralph. They prayed for me, and I am totally healed."

I asked if I could lay my hand on his back, which he agreed to, and then I prayed a simple prayer, "Lord, let Your presence come on his back. Bring Your Kingdom. I speak alignment in Jesus' name." I asked if he felt anything going on, and he said that he felt heat in his lower back where I had placed my hand.

I followed up by asking him to do something that he could not do, like touch his toes. At first he was hesitant, but through the encouragement of his wife and the rest of the team, he decided to make an attempt. As he cautiously began to bend over to appease us, he suddenly realized that he had no more pain, and that instead he had complete flexibility. He began to touch the ground over and over, bending with ease. He was totally healed. Then Ralph also prayed to invite Jesus into his life. Two treasures had been found!

Risk Releases ROI

Taking risk is like an investment. Most of us approach a potential investment, consider the risk, and then weigh it against the potential "return on investment," or ROI. Quite often, the ROI is commensurate to the level of risk—the higher the level of risk, the greater potential for a high return. Therefore, the very fact that an activity carries a certain amount of risk reveals that the potential return on that risk may be well worth the investment.

When Christians invest what God has provided, He promises that the return on that investment will be rewarded with increase. In the parable of the talents, Jesus makes the point that if we take risk to invest what we have been given, then more will be added to us (see Matt. 25:14-30). In other words, we get a great return on our investments in the Kingdom when we take risk.

We cannot get a return on something we do not invest in. In other words—no risk yields no reward. Like the fearful servant who took his one talent and hid it, we will not only miss out on our supernatural destiny, but we will also lose everything we have held onto in fear. The confidence we have in God's promises to provide for us will determine the amount of risk we are willing to take in putting everything on the line.

The Purpose of Faith

In Hebrews 11:1, faith is defined as being sure of what we hope for and certain of what we do not see. The more confident we are in God's promises, the more likely we are to take risks.

In Revelation 22:12, Jesus promised that He would be coming soon, and that He would reward each person according to what he or she had done. By investing in the things of the Kingdom, we can be sure of a great reward.

I believe that keeping the faith is contingent upon keeping our eye on the reward. Similarly, when I am confident that God will release His supernatural resources as I step out in a lifestyle of risk, I find myself making continual investments.

Often, I will take a risk to release healing on people when I am out in the community, going about my day. Each time I step out, I find myself going through an analysis process that goes something like this: "I'm going to look foolish and incompetent if they do not get healed!" Then, I will remember all of the miracles I have seen when I took risks in the past, and I will conclude, "OK, I'll take the risk. It is worth the potential embarrassment to obtain the reward of seeing people healed."

Taking the risk to release the supernatural Kingdom of God opens up the possibility for the miraculous. Risk is an investment of faith that releases the supernatural Kingdom of God in people's lives and circumstances.

Most people do not take risks because they lack confidence that God will come through on His end of the partnership. What if He doesn't show up? But the longer you take risks and step out on what you feel God is showing you, the more you will discover that God is faithful. When you take a risk, He comes.

Abraham is a classic example of one who focused on the reward of his risk. The writer to the Hebrews tells us that,

> By faith Abraham, even though he was past age—and Sarah herself was barren—was enabled to become a father because he considered him faithful who had made the promise. And so from this one man, and he as good as dead, came descendants as numerous as the stars in the sky and as countless as the sand on the seashore (Hebrews 11:11-12 NIV 1984).

If we truly believe God is able to do the impossible, then, like Abraham, we will determine to ride upon the prophetic promises that God has given us to carry out. We will live in the hope that God is faithful to provide what we need to bring about the promise that our risk is releasing. We will not worry about the details. That is God's job.

Let's Talk About It

What risks did you take yesterday and today? Talk about why they were risks for you, even if others might not consider them to be risks. How did God come through for you? How can you be more intentional about stepping out in risk?

_____
_____
_____
_____
_____
_____
_____
_____
_____
_____
_____
_____
_____
_____
_____
_____
_____
_____
_____
_____
_____
_____
_____
_____
_____
_____

Taking Risks in Haiti

I was in Haiti a few weeks after the earthquake devastated the capital city of Port au Prince in January 2010. One day, we were ministering in a small suburban community looking for people who needed medical help. We had several nurses and doctors on our team, as well as those who were solely equipped with faith to believe for supernatural intervention to heal the sick and the injured and to raise the dead.

We came to a place where the UN troops had just dropped off rice, beans, and water. An angry crowd had formed next to one of the dilapidated buildings. At first we thought a fight was breaking out over the distribution of the food and water, but we soon learned that the commotion was over a woman who had just collapsed and died on the side of the dirt road.

It was obvious that the crowd had seen enough death. They were expressing their anger over this woman who had survived the earthquake only to collapse and die due to undetected internal injuries she received during the quake. It felt as if the yelling, fist-pumping crowd was at a tipping point of disappointment; they seemed to be on the brink of rioting.

Something came over me as I approached the mob. I turned to my team and exclaimed, "Let's go raise her from the dead!" They nodded back their support of the bold risk I was about to take in the midst of the volatile crowd surrounding the dead woman. Before fear had an opportunity to dissuade me from my seeming stupidity, I began yelling, "Medical, medical...." Amazingly, the crowd parted as our medical doctor held up his stethoscope as a sign that we were there to help. Everyone was silent as our doctor confirmed what the crowd already knew—the woman was indeed dead.

I could sense the rising rage in reaction to the news, as it was passed throughout the crowd. At that moment, I decided that I needed to change the atmosphere before the crowd turned on us in violence. Throwing all caution to the wind, I yelled out, "Who wants to see this woman raised from the dead?" They all erupted with approving cheers.

I could see in their eyes that they were desperate for something good to happen, so I began to prophesy that it was time for life in Haiti, and that God was going to reveal His goodness to them. Once again, the crowd responded in ecstatic unison, as they began to shout, "Vive, vive, vive!" Live, live, live!

The team and I began to declare life into the woman, as the crowd looked on with hopeful anticipation. We were so full of faith, but after about thirty minutes, I could sense that the crowd was becoming restless and losing hope. So I decided to change the atmosphere again. While the rest of the team continued praying for the dead woman to come back to life, I began to call out words of knowledge for ailments represented in particular people in the crowd.

Healings started breaking out throughout the crowd as each word of knowledge was acknowledged. Over the next forty-five minutes, the team and I continued calling out words of knowledge, and many more were healed. A blind woman got healed. Another woman had a cancerous tumor dissolve.

A guy came up to the crowd riding a bicycle. After observing our revival outbreak for a few minutes, he began yelling, "f*** you," over and over, while extending one finger of his right hand. Over his obvious disdain, I shouted out a word of knowledge for someone with a torn rotator cuff. Immediately, the man's right hand retracted, covering his left shoulder. He looked at me in dismay, as his left rotator cuff had been completely healed!

We did not see the breakthrough we were expecting for the woman who had died, but as we attempted to lift 1,000 pounds, so to speak, we were able to see amazing miracles of the 500-pound variety because we took risk to go to the next extreme level.

Risk is the spark that ignites the fire of God's passion to be released in, and through, our lives. Jesus said, "Truly I tell you, if you have faith as small as a mustard seed, you can say to this mountain, 'Move from here to there,' and it will move. Nothing will be impossible for you" (Matt. 17:20). Like an out-of-control wildfire that is ignited by a tiny strike of a match, even the smallest level of risk also ignites miraculous breakthrough.

Let's Receive It

I release you into the next levels of risk—so that you would be able to cross the chicken line, leading to new adventures and breakthrough in bringing Heaven to earth on behalf of others. I pray that you would have complete confidence that when you take risk, God will come, and that when He comes, He will do good things because He is a good God in a good mood.

Let's Do It!

1.) Give each member of the group a word of encouragement. Try to get words of knowledge about each member of the group.

2.) Determine your next level of risk and make an action plan to do it by the next meeting. (Write down how it went—How did you feel? What was the outcome?—and so forth.) Be prepared to share your risk adventure with the group at the beginning of your next meeting.

— Week —
THREE

Empowered by Joy: Learning to Laugh Launches a Lifestyle of Revival

Prior to speaking at a conference, God gave me the name "Rhonda" and the word "lupus" as a word of knowledge. I wrote the two words down on my teaching notes. Before I began to launch into the subject that I was teaching that evening, I asked if a Rhonda was present. I asked a few times, but no one responded, so I went on with my message, wondering why Rhonda had not responded.

About ten minutes into my teaching, however, I could not get "Rhonda" off my mind, so I stopped to ask one more time, "There has to be a Rhonda here—is there a Rhonda here?"

One of the elders sitting in the second row sheepishly raised his hand and confessed that his wife was named Rhonda, but that she was at home sick.

"Get her on the cell phone," I insisted.

Once he got her on the phone, he handed the phone to me. I introduced myself and explained the word of knowledge that I had received prior to the meeting.

I asked if there was a possibility that she had lupus. At that, she burst into tears, along with her husband in the second row. As she continued crying over the phone, her husband explained to the congregation that Rhonda had been diagnosed with lupus that very week and was at home in terrible pain. She had not told anyone in the church because she was so depressed over the prognosis that she would never recover. There is no medical cure for lupus.

I began to share with Rhonda that God had a different prognosis, that He had highlighted her to show her that He wanted to heal her. With that knowledge, she began to laugh hysterically through the cell phone, which prompted me to laugh. I put her on speakerphone, and as her laughter belted into the auditorium, the entire congregation erupted in spontaneous laughter.

After laughing for about ten minutes, I asked how she was feeling. Through bursts of laughter, she shared that all of the pain had left, starting with her arms and finishing with her legs. She was completely healed.

The next morning, she came to both church services to testify of the healing and demonstrate her glowing countenance. She also shared that she and her husband had spent a few hours laughing together upon his return that night. When the Kingdom shows up, joy comes too—and anything is possible.

Overflowing Joy

In John 17, Jesus prays six things for the disciples. He prays that they will be protected (see John 17:11, 15), that they will be sanctified (see John 17:17-19), that they will be unified (see John 17:20-23), that they will have His glory (see John 17:24), that they will experience His presence (see John 17:24), and that they will encounter His love (see John 17:26).

To sum up, Jesus prays, "I say these things [the six things He is praying for]...so that they may have the full measure of my joy within them" (John 17:13). The goal of being sanctified, protected, and unified, of having God's glory and experiencing His presence and love, is that we will have all of the joy that Jesus carries.

The question is: How much joy does Jesus have? How much is a "full measure"? Does He just have enough for one person, one event, or one circumstance? Does He just have enough for one season of life? Is His measure equivalent to a gallon, a water truck, a lake, or an ocean?

Jesus' joy is limitless. His joy is eternal, everlasting. Therefore, it is immeasurable. A full measure of Jesus' joy will never run out. There is a constant supply. *That* is the very measure that Jesus is praying would be in us—an unending, limitless, everlasting supply of joy.

So then, what happens when His container of immeasurable joy flows into us? Just as David put it in his best-loved psalm, we will be able to say, "My cup overflows" (Ps. 23:5). Imagine God's limitless measure of joy as a liter-sized bottle, and imagine your container size, designed to hold this joy, as the little bottle cap. What would happen if you poured the entire liter of liquid into the cap? It would run over.

When His limitless measure comes into our finite container, naturally it overflows. We simply cannot contain the full measure of God's joy; it must leak out of us like streams of living water.

So in essence, Jesus was praying that we would be filled continuously with so much joy that, wherever we went, we would leak on everyone around us. This is one of the keys to releasing the Kingdom of God. It is a key to living a naturally supernatural life. His overflowing joy can literally change the world around us.

Let's Talk About It

Do you feel that you or anybody you know carries a full measure of God's joy—or at least a growing measure of joy? What would that look like, practically, in your life? How would people know that you had a full measure?

When Abraham and Sarah were given the promise that a nation would be birthed through them, even though they were way past their ability to have children, they laughed at the notion. "Abraham fell facedown; he laughed and said to himself, 'Will a son be born to a man a hundred years old? Will Sarah bear a child at the age of ninety?'" (Gen. 17:17). "Sarah laughed to herself as she thought, 'After I am worn out and my lord is old, will I now have this pleasure?'" (Gen. 18:12). I believe they laughed because they knew that they could not bring about their destiny in their own strength. The very thought was ludicrous and amusing to them.

Notice that God does not scold them for laughing. In Sarah's case, God simply points out that she laughed. Even when Sarah denies it, there is no punishment or correction, just an acknowledgement of the laughter in the face of the impossibility (see Gen. 18:13-15). In addition, God does not even mention Abraham's laughter in response to the impossible destiny that He was to fulfill.

In fact, both of them were inducted into the "Faith Hall of Fame" in Hebrews 11 for believing against all odds. Abraham's laughter did not mean that he did not have faith. The apostle Paul states: "Abraham believed God, and it was credited to him as righteousness" (Rom. 4:3).

Paul then goes on to say:

Against all hope, Abraham in hope believed and so became the father of many nations, just as it had been said to him…. Without weakening in his faith, he faced the fact that his body was as good as dead—since he was about a hundred years old—and that Sarah's womb was also dead. Yet he did not waver through unbelief regarding the promise of God, but was strengthened in his faith and gave glory to God, being fully persuaded that God had power to do what he had promised. This is why "it was credited to him as righteousness" (Romans 4:18-22).

It seems that laughter is an appropriate response to impossible promises and circumstances. Moreover, I believe that laughter is a primary key that unlocks Heaven and releases the Kingdom in and through our lives. In Nehemiah 8:10, we are told that the joy of the Lord is our strength. A synonym for strength is "empowerment." The power of the Kingdom of God is fueled by joy.

If we want to be world-changers, we must have a higher source of power operating in and through our lives. That source is God's presence, where there is fullness of joy (see Ps. 16:11). A river does not have to work hard to bring water into valleys. It simply flows from a higher source. In the same way, releasing the Kingdom means simply allowing the river of joy to flow through us from Heaven, bringing Heaven to earth.

I remember one time I was laughing by myself in my car. I was stopped at a red light, and I looked over at the woman in the car next to me. Without knowing what I was laughing about, she began to laugh with me through the closed windows. If the light had not turned to green, I really think I could have led her to Christ because of the instant rapport we had in a common laugh. There have been so many times I have disarmed even the most hardened cynic with a smile, and as a result, gained entrance into his life for a divine appointment.

Joy Is Normal

One-third of the Kingdom of God is joy. How do I know that? Because I read in Romans 14:17 that "The kingdom of God is not a matter of eating and drinking, but of righteousness, peace and joy in the Holy Spirit." In other words, the Kingdom of God consists of three things, and joy is one of them. Joy is one of the primary characteristics of the Kingdom of God because joy is one of the primary characteristics of the King.

So then, when the Kingdom comes, joy is to be expected. It is normal to experience joy in God's presence. Jesus taught His disciples to pray, "…on earth as it is in heaven" (Matt. 6:10). If Heaven is filled with joy, it only makes sense that earth should be filled with joy as well. Even the angels rejoice when one sinner repents (see Luke 15:10), which implies that there is a constant party of joy in Heaven because people on earth are constantly coming into right relationship with God. Before Jesus spoke that line, He told the story of the woman who found her lost coin, and something about that story always reminds me of a treasure hunt!

Joy should be the normal mood for a Christian. We see in Galatians 5:22 that joy is an important part of the fruit of the Spirit. This is because joy should be a natural outgrowth of living in the Spirit, which is the same as living in God's presence. Joy should be cultivated as a daily lifestyle; it should be a continual occurrence, not just a once-in-a-while event. Paul commanded the Thessalonians to be joyful always (see 1 Thess. 5:16).

He also wrote to the Christians at Philippi—from prison, which is normally not a very joyful place—encouraging them with these words: "Rejoice in the Lord always. [And, just in case you did not get it the first time] I will say it again: Rejoice" (Phil. 4:4). In other words, keep being joyful, over and over again. God intends for His righteous ones to be filled with joy and laughter.

Let's Talk About It

What role has joy played in your Christian experience? How have you used joy and laughter as a resource of strength and empowerment in releasing the Kingdom of God to others?

_____

_____

_____

_____

_____

_____

_____

_____

_____

_____

_____

_____

_____

_____

_____

_____

_____

_____

_____

_____

_____

_____

_____

_____

_____

In the midst of Job's depressing trials, Bildad attempted to comfort him with this promise: "Surely God does not reject one who is blameless or strengthen the hands of evildoers. He will yet fill your mouth with laughter and your lips with shouts of joy" (Job 8:20-21).

When the Galatian Christians, influenced by false teachers, were considering returning to the Law of Judaism in order to escape the persecution that came from their identification with Christ, Paul's response was an interesting one. Instead of correcting their theology, he asked, in essence, "What has happened to all your joy?" (see Gal. 4:15). He was saying, in other words, that they had forfeited their joy when they decided to revert to the religious restrictions of the Law, and if they were claiming to be in right relationship with God, they should not be so sad.

When David repented over his sin with Bathsheba, he was concerned with only two things. First, he prayed that God would not cast him from His presence or take the Holy Spirit from him, and second, he prayed that his joy of salvation would be restored (see Ps. 51:11-12).

Isaiah prophesied that the Messiah, the Christ, would bring the oil of gladness and everlasting joy (see Isa. 61:3, 7). When the angel of the Lord announced the birth of Jesus, he said, "I bring you good news of great joy that will be for all the people" (Luke 2:10 NIV 1984). Even before Jesus was born, Mary went to visit her cousin Elizabeth, and as soon as John, the unborn child still in Elizabeth's womb, encountered the unborn Jesus, who was still in Mary's womb, John leaped for joy (see Luke 1:41)! In Luke 6:21b, Jesus announced, "Blessed [literally, "Hugely happy"] are you who weep now [before the Kingdom comes], for [when the Kingdom comes] you will laugh."

When Jesus shows up, joy will be the normal response. No wonder we see healings and new life along with overflowing joy. Jesus Himself is in that place and His Kingdom of joy has come.

The Church should be the happiest place on planet Earth. The Church should be the place where people can truly find "happy hour." A fast-food restaurant should not be the only place that offers a "happy meal." The Church should be the place where people can laugh in the freedom of God's presence. The Church should be attractive to others, because of the joy expressed by the people.

Those of us who are believers should experience the joy of the Kingdom of God on a continual basis. It should be normal for us to spread the Kingdom of joy wherever we go, as we desire to see Heaven on earth.

Holy Disorder

Some people worry about laughter in the Church getting out of order. Without a doubt, it can get out of order, but so can singing, prophecy, tongues, dancing, and on and on. We are not supposed to discontinue these things just because there is a possibility of disorder. We are to pastor them.

I would add too that our sense of order might be very different from God's sense of order. We tend to think that order means sameness and predictability. Our orderliness puts everything in nice, neat rows, at 90-degree angles, and is perfectly level. God's sense of order is mountains popping up all over the place and winding rivers and trees strewn every which way with no semblance of purpose. A short pine tree grows next to a towering fir tree. No two individual people look exactly the same. In creation, almost nothing is level; there are very few 90-degree angles; nice, neat rows are a rarity. We do see those things, but they have come from a human sense of order. God's sense of order can look pretty messy and disorderly from our perspective. We often misjudge something God is doing, because it doesn't meet our standards of propriety.

Remember what happened when the Ark of the Covenant (i.e., the presence of God) was returned to Israel (see 2 Sam. 6)? David got pretty wild and crazy in his celebration. His wife, Michal, looked on the scene with disdain, as she believed David's exuberant behavior was beneath his dignity. David's response is insightful: "It was before the Lord…I will celebrate before the Lord. I will become even more undignified than this, and I will be humiliated in my own eyes…" (2 Sam. 6:21-22).

David helps us appreciate our delightfully human ability to laugh. Some believers are afraid that the flesh will get out of control when there is too much laughter. They may refer to spiritual laughter as "holy laughter," as though they want to distinguish between laughing "in the Spirit" (impelled by God's Spirit) and laughing "in the flesh" (laughter that is of human origin). Notice what David wrote: "My soul longed and even yearned for the courts of the Lord; my heart and *my flesh* sing for joy to the living God" (Ps. 84:2 NASB).

When God generates our laughter, our natural human flesh is involved. How could it not be? And that laughter affects everything, bringing with it all the benefits of Heaven.

The sad thing about this joy is that joy is *not* a normal lifestyle for many Christians. Solemn teachers instruct us that laughter is inappropriate within the sacred precincts of the church sanctuary, although weeping is all right, because it may indicate that the Spirit is moving. Uncontrolled laughter might be viewed as immature and out of order in a church service, but if someone cries throughout a message, we consider it an appropriate, deeply felt response.

As children, most of us were told to stop laughing in public settings and to act like adults. "OK," we thought. "Mature people do not laugh uncontrollably. Laughter expresses an emotion, and emotions are hard to control." The only exception is that we should laugh in response to the pastor's good joke told from the pulpit. Can't we see that it's inherently wrong to limit the joy of the Lord to a well-timed joke?

Let's Talk About It

What is your experience of Spirit-impelled laughter? Why is it hard to separate "holy laughter" from natural laughter? Do we always need to distinguish between those two kinds of laughter? Why or why not?

Laughter Is a Choice

We have developed an underlying mindset that Christians are not supposed to live by feelings, but rather "by faith." Although it's true that my feelings should not affect my faith, the converse is not true. My faith *should* affect my feelings. If I have put my faith in the God of the impossible, then my joy should be infectious. Because of my abiding faith, I should be able to live in joy and happiness under any circumstance.

Even if I do not feel happy, I can choose by faith to laugh through any hardship, based on the truth that God is always good, despite my circumstances. It's not insincere to do so—because it's the truth!

The fact is that laughter is a choice. If we have enough self-control, we can stop laughing, so by the same token we should be able to choose to start laughing whenever we want to. (Self-control, part of the fruit of the Spirit listed in Galatians 5:23, should be characterized by choosing to do the good, not just abstaining from the bad.)

Furthermore, like any other fruit of the Spirit, self-control and joy must be cultivated in order to grow. Without cultivation, they will not be in evidence in our daily lives. We cultivate joy by cultivating our relationship with the Holy Spirit. Even Jesus cultivated joy as He accessed Heaven through the Holy Spirit. Luke tells us that Jesus was "full of joy through the Holy Spirit" (Luke 10:21).

Joy Comes in the Mourning

Certainly, crying, sorrow, and mourning are a part of life, but it is not God's goal for us to remain there. Solomon observed: "There is a time for everything…a time to weep and a time to laugh…" (Eccles. 3:1, 4). Although we are encouraged to mourn with those who mourn (see Rom. 12:15), crying is not meant to last. It is not normal for a believer to spend his or her whole life in sadness. In Psalm 30:5, David provided hope with these words: "…weeping may stay for the night, but rejoicing [joy] comes in the morning."

In the context of reaching out to the world around us, we should view dire needs and sorrowful circumstances as perfect opportunities for the Spirit of God. In the midst of impossibly difficult situations, a display of His power and love doubles the rejoicing.

God is always in a good mood, and He wants to share the joy and laughter with us. I have a picture on a shelf in my office depicting Jesus laughing, which constantly reminds me of His mood toward me. Throughout the day, as I happen to glance at it, I am overwhelmed with a sense of supernatural strengthen as I remember that "…the joy of the Lord is my strength" (see Neh. 8:10). In other words, when we encounter His joy, an empowering comes, not only internally, but also in the releasing of miracles.

When you and I are able to picture His good mood toward us, it releases the supernatural Kingdom in and through our lives. This is even more the case when we pursue the Giver of the river of living water and drink Him in so that we are sure to overflow. We can minister very effectively to the people around us out of our experience with a joyful God.

Let's Talk About It

Does it surprise you that so many Scriptures speak directly about joy? Why do you think this subject has been so overlooked in the teaching of the Church? Can you think of other topics that were overlooked throughout Church history? How do you think we can restore the power of joy back to the Church?

Here's a good example of what I mean. During the time of worship at a church where I had been invited to speak, a woman came through a door to the right of the stage. She was hooked up to an oxygen tank on wheels, which her husband was pushing behind her, and her three children, walking in single file, followed her.

It took what seemed like forever for her to make it halfway to the front row, where I was sitting with the ministry team that I had brought. She was struggling at each step, and I found myself rooting for her to make it to a chair. By the time she got to the crowded front row, I could not bear watching her labor any longer. I offered our seats, which she and her family gladly accepted, and I stood next to her on the end seat, continuing to worship.

I had been drinking in the Spirit all morning, and as I stood next to the woman, that living water began to overflow. Without giving her any greeting, without even knowing what was wrong with her, I put my hand on her head and spontaneously erupted into laughter. (This is not the way that I normally begin a time of ministry, but because I was "drunk in the Spirit," I lost all sense of protocol.)

Immediately I could feel her head bobbing up and down as she began laughing hysterically. We continued to laugh, still without a proper introduction. After a few minutes, she jumped out of her chair, pulled the oxygen tubes out of her nostrils, and sucked in the atmosphere, filling her lungs to capacity.

She breathed out the air that she had inhaled and looked at me with surprise. Not knowing her medical condition, I gave her a look that said, "OK, you can breathe—that's good…." Recognizing that I did not understand the significance of her breathing feat, she explained that she had not been able to breathe like that in years. She further explained that she had been in and out of hospitals over the past few years and that she had nearly died several times. Moreover, even though she had gone to specialist after specialist, no one could diagnose the problem. Out of frustration, they finally termed her condition "a failure to thrive."

She had racked up over a million dollars in co-payments alone, and still she had no hope for breakthrough. The day before, she had been released from the hospital where she had been treated for a severe case of pneumonia, the effects of which she was still suffering from. She was supposed to be on complete bed rest, but she felt that she just had to get to church that morning.

She ran over to the pastors and repeated the same breathing demonstration she had performed for me. The pastors looked on with wide eyes of excitement as the woman took off running across the front of the auditorium. She then picked up a flag and began running, jumping, and dancing to the roar of the congregation, who all were quite aware of her medical condition. I found out later that most of the church had been taking turns caring for her and her family over the previous two years with meals, housekeeping, and emotional support.

The pastor asked her to share her testimony, in which she exclaimed that all of the pain in her body had left and that her lungs had been completely restored. Six months later, the husband sent word through the pastor, thanking me for leaking joy on his wife. They now have their lives back, and all I did was laugh with her!

Supernatural Joy = Supernatural Power

From experiences such as that one, I have learned that as I operate out of His supernatural joy, I am filled with supernatural power that can heal the sick and set the captives free. David put it clearly when he said, "Splendor and majesty are before him; strength and joy are in his dwelling place" (1 Chron. 16:27). In the second psalm, we are told that "the One enthroned in heaven laughs" (Ps. 2:4). In this context, God is laughing in response to the plots and plans of the enemy to thwart the purposes of God. It's as if He is saying, "Are you joking? Do you really think you're going to win? That's funny!" If God's response is to laugh at the enemy's tactics, then how much more effective could we be in destroying the works of the devil if we laugh, too?

I probably don't have to tell you that we laugh a lot when we are doing treasure hunts. You have to believe that when your life is overflowing with the joy of Jesus, leaking new life all over the place, it is as enjoyable as it gets!

 ## Let's Receive It

I pray that you would encounter the laughter of Heaven in your everyday life. I release the grace to use your fruit of self-control to choose laughter by faith, even when you don't feel like it. May you be able to see and hear His laughter over you as you encounter His good mood toward you. As you align yourself more and more with the joy of the Lord, may you find the supernatural empowerment you need to release His presence and power to those around you who need to encounter His good mood.

Let's Do It!

1.) Practice laughing with your group. (It may feel awkward and strange at first.) Don't stop! Try to go at least ten minutes. How do you feel? Was or is it hard for you to feel comfortable laughing? Explain.

2.) Purpose to laugh as you go through your week. Share your journey of joy with the group next week.

— W e e k —

FOUR

You Have What It Takes!
Fostering Relationship with
the Father Fuels the Fire of Revival

After an intense weekend of ministry in another church, I was driving home in a van with my wife and our student ministry team. We stopped for gas at a gas station that had a mini-mart in the middle of nowhere north of Sacramento, California. Our whole team (far from being out of fuel themselves, even though they had had a long weekend), piled out of the vehicle to see what treasures the Lord had hidden in this unlikely location at ten o'clock at night.

Before I had finished filling the gas tank, I could see that most of them had found somebody to talk with. Two of our students asked a truck driver to test the healing of his back pain. I saw my wife and two other students smiling with delight as a couple of people by the entrance of the mini-mart flexed their knees and necks in response to God's healing touch. At least two other students were inside the mini-mart, and I was pretty sure that they were not just buying snacks.

Suddenly, a woman with a mini-mart uniform came out with a concerned look on her face. She spotted me and immediately began walking toward me. My first thought was, *Oh great, here we go. She is probably mad about the mini revival that has just broken out in her mini-mart.*

As she reached me, she asked if I was the leader of the group who had just invaded her mini-mart. I sheepishly responded in the affirmative, bracing myself for a rebuke. To my surprise, however, she was not mad at all. Still with a concerned look on her face, she related her reason for approaching me.

She explained that she had been to the doctor that morning and had been informed that she had cervical cancer. She had a husband and two young girls at home and could not muster the courage to tell them. Now her shift was nearly over, and she did not know how she was going to break the bad news. Even though she was not a Christian, when she saw all of the people being healed inside and outside of the mini-mart, she began to think that we could help her.

She went on to say that she did not want to say anything inside the store because a local person could come in and overhear the conversation and possibly leak the information to her family before she had the courage to tell them herself. With that in mind, she had asked where the leader of our group was, and the students inside directed her to me.

I called one of our female students over to help me minister to the woman, and we immediately began to call out her destiny through prophetic words. We then began to pray for her, with laughter and proclamations of God's goodness. After a few minutes, she looked up with tear-soaked eyes and explained that she had felt "butterfly" sensations going through her cervix. After we were done blessing her, she thanked us profusely for stopping at her mini-mart.

Eventually all of us got back into the van and headed home, having become personally aware of a greater meaning of the term, "filling station."

Doing What the Father Is Doing

God was gathering up a lot of treasures that night in the gas station, as we simply tried to track with what He wanted us to do, in effect "doing what the Father was doing."

In John 5:19, we are told that Jesus could only do what He saw His Father doing because whatever the Father did the Son also did. For a long time I used to think that Jesus must have had to stop in the midst of His daily activities and everyday encounters with people and ask, "Father, what are You doing here?"

I assumed that Jesus would have had to spot-check each encounter. "Father, do You want to heal this person? Do You want Me to prophesy to this person? Do You want Me to help this person?" I figured He must have gotten His answers quickly, but I took for granted that Jesus would not release the Kingdom unless He got a green light, case by case, from His Father.

I changed my mind after I thought about the woman who had an issue of blood who touched the hem of Jesus' robe (see Luke 8:43-48). When that happened, Jesus didn't stop and say, "Hold it, woman, we need to ask the Father whether or not He wants to do this right now." No, the woman touched His clothing and drew out the power resident within Him through faith. She didn't ask; she just grabbed what was already available in Jesus.

At the same time, Jesus certainly did only what His Father was doing. So the question becomes whether this is manifested on a case-by-case basis or as an ongoing lifestyle.

I want to propose that the Father has already given us a green light to release the Kingdom to anyone, wherever we go. The fact is that our Father in Heaven is always healing, and we know this because one of His names is Yahweh Rapha—"the Lord who heals you" (see Exod. 15:26). This reflects His nature, character, attributes, actions, and will. The Father's name never changes, so His will never changes.

The Father does not sit in Heaven thinking, "All right, I'm healing…you…you…and you…but not you." No, because of His nature, God's will is to heal everyone. He is always releasing healing virtue from Heaven. It is up to us to administrate it on earth.

Jesus healed wherever He went because He always saw His Father healing from Heaven. Jesus did not have special times in which He healed people, prophesied, or set them free. It wasn't like He had a healing conference where people would sign up for the chance to be touched. No, He walked through a crowd, and when the woman with the hemorrhage came into contact with Him, she was healed. It was that natural. We also read of people being healed as Peter's shadow covered them because he carried the same Kingdom presence as Jesus (see Acts 5:14-16).

Jesus lived a naturally supernatural lifestyle. Scripture tells us that "God anointed Jesus of Nazareth with the Holy Spirit and power…because God was with him" (Acts 10:38).

We have the same anointing that Jesus received, because we have received the same Holy Spirit, who continues to anoint and empower believers today. Therefore, we have the same obligation to do only what the Father is doing today—just as He was doing in His Son Jesus' time on earth.

Let's Talk About It

When you stop and think about it, have you also assumed that Jesus must have somehow silently consulted the Father every single time He did something? What difference does it make in your daily life to realize that He didn't—and that His heavenly power and will to love others everywhere is always resident in you?

Relationship, Not Religion

"Doing what the Father is doing" implies a relationship. It doesn't mean "doing what you *ought* to be doing" or following a system of rules and regulations. We can only do what our Father is doing if we value intimacy more than performance and resting in Him more than striving to please Him. We put faith over formula and relationship over religion.

Jesus taught His disciples that bringing Heaven to earth in order to do God's will flows from intimately knowing God as "our Father." In other words, a true understanding of God as our Father—my very own Father—is a primary key to living a naturally supernatural life. No treasure hunter should leave home without it.

Jesus instructed His disciples to pray in the secret place to "your Father" (see Matt, 6:6). He was teaching them an entirely new way to pray. There is a noticeable difference between the Jewish religious prayers and the prayer model that Jesus taught the disciples. The Jews always addressed God as "*the* Father" in the Amidah and Kaddish (both of which, by the way, are very similar to the prayer here in Matthew 6), while Jesus practiced and taught His disciples to address God as "*our* Father."

This idea, the thought of addressing God as "our Father," was a huge deal in Jewish religious culture. The Jews considered it blasphemous to say that God was your father. That is why the religious leaders wanted to kill Jesus: "…he was even calling God his own Father, making himself equal with God" (John 5:18).

To the Jews, God was the Father of all creation; He was the originator of humankind and everything else in the world. Therefore, to call him "the Father" signified a transcendent relationship between God and human beings. And to claim that God was your own personal Father meant that you were not of human origin, but in fact, equal to God.

On the other hand, Jews considered Abraham to be their father. As the originator of Israel, it was similar to the way that we refer to George Washington as one of the founding fathers of the United States of America. Likewise, they considered Adam, as the first man, to be the father of humankind. This did not bother them, because they remained children of humanity, children of human fathers; those fathers had human origins.

Then Jesus came along, demonstrating no hesitation in calling God His very own Father. He knew who His Daddy was. By calling God His own Father, He was specifying that He was of divine origin and therefore not from this world. This was utterly true, and it offended and infuriated the pharisaical Jews.

Thanks to Jesus, we have come to realize that we are "children born not of natural descent, nor of human decision or a husband's will, but born of God" (John 1:13). Thus, like Jesus, we too are now of divine origin. We are literally God's children, and we have all of the rights and privileges that go along with that status. It was with that understanding that Jesus taught His disciples to pray "our Father," "my Father...."

Let's Talk About It

Talk about your experience of relating to God as *my* Father instead of *the* Father. Why do you think it is so important to know God as *our* Father, *my* Father?

_____

_____

_____

_____

_____

_____

_____

_____

_____

_____

_____

_____

_____

_____

_____

_____

_____

_____

_____

_____

_____

_____

_____

_____

_____

Identity Gives Access and Access Gives Intimacy

When we know God as *our* Father versus the Father, then we will know who we are as His children, and we will begin to understand our identity.

Out of our identity as His children, we find access to Him. Out of access to Him, we find intimacy with Him. Out of intimacy with Him, we have the authority to release what we have accessed. And our authority results in influence—"Your kingdom come, your will be done" (Matt. 6:10). This all begins in knowing God as "our Father."

Otherwise, we will only relate to Him as a servant relates to his master, and servants do not have the same privileges as sons and daughters. In John 15:15, Jesus said, "I no longer call you servants, because a servant does not know his master's business. Instead, I have called you friends, for everything that I learned from my Father I have made known to you." John gives a greater revelation when he points out that we are the children of God (see 1 John 3:1). The apostle Paul confirms this reality in Romans 8:16 when he writes, "The Spirit himself testifies with our spirit that we are God's children." Furthermore, in Galatians 4:1-7, Paul speaks of the inheritance that we have as children, reminding us that we do not have to wait to obtain it, because Jesus has already died.

Moving Heaven to Earth

So having access to the Father is the key to being able to bring Heaven to earth, whether we are actively treasure hunting or just praying as we wash the dishes.

Moreover, Jesus was not teaching His disciples to offer up a hopeful plea for God's Kingdom and will to be done on earth as it is in Heaven. I used to pray, "O Father, (let/may) Your Kingdom come, Your will be done...." That is, until I discovered that the verbs in Greek are in the declarative mood. The declarative mood indicates that Jesus was urging us to declare God's will be done rather than ask for His will to be done. Jesus was not teaching His disciples to plead for the power of the Father to show up, but rather to declare His presence and power into the circumstances and environment that needed His intervention!

So then, wherever we go we are to be distributors of His Kingdom. In a real sense, Jesus was teaching the disciples that as sons, they now had the authority and the responsibility to release the Kingdom of God—God's will—on the earth. In that light, many Christians continually ask God to do what He has already empowered them to do! The fact is our declarations make a difference in bringing Heaven to earth in supernatural ways.

We are the children of God (see 1 John 3:1), which means we are to be identified with His name. We are called Christians because we have taken His name. Our job is to bring God's Kingdom to earth, which means that we represent His name. Therefore, we have the power associated with the name we carry, power that enables us to meet any need we may encounter.

Let's Talk About It

Do you believe—really believe and act on—the fact that you can bring Heaven to earth? Is your belief in the theoretical realm, or have you proved it? If you have proved it by your actions, what did you do and what was the result?

My Son, Whom I Love

Besides having access to the Father, another key to the ability to release physical healing is living and operating in the truth of our sonship.

When Jesus was being baptized by John the Baptist, the Holy Spirit descended upon Him and the Father spoke audibly from Heaven saying, "This is my Son, whom I love; with him I am well pleased" (Matt. 3:17). This statement is a public declaration of Jesus' identity as the Son of God.

Before this event, we have no record of Jesus demonstrating supernatural ministry. It was not until He was baptized, received the Spirit, and heard the pronouncement from His Father that He performed His first miracle of turning water into wine while at Cana (see John 2:11). Peter, in Acts 10:38, explained that it was the anointing of the Spirit that enabled Jesus to heal. But I believe that the Father's words spoken at Jesus' baptism were just as crucial to releasing the supernatural Kingdom through His life.

In Jewish tradition, it was customary for a father to bring his eldest son to a public place (normally the city gates where business and judicial decisions were transacted), put his arm around him, and proclaim to the "powers that be" that his son now possessed full authority to transact family business on his behalf. Upon that declaration, the son had the right to buy or sell anything in the family business as if the father were conducting the transaction himself. From that point on, he had complete authority and empowerment as a son. Whatever the son said was said as though the father had said it himself. The son's words carried the father's authority, which is why declaration is so vital to the treasure hunter. "We are therefore Christ's ambassadors, as though God were making his appeal through us" (2 Cor. 5:20a).

In the same way, the Father spoke from Heaven at His Son's baptism, proclaiming to the world that His Son, Jesus, was now authorized to transact Kingdom business on His behalf. His empowerment came through the anointing of the Holy Spirit, and it also came through His recognized identity as a son.

I would suggest that many Christians who have long been empowered by the Holy Spirit, but who have been frustrated in their efforts to heal the sick, should take a deep look into understanding the full meaning of the sonship or daughterhood they enjoy with their Father. This may be the missing key to opening many treasures.

Besides telling His disciples that they were now His friends, not His servants, Jesus added, "You did not choose me, but I chose you and appointed you so that you might go and bear fruit—fruit that will last—and so that whatever you ask in my name the Father will give you" (John 15:16). The disciples (and by extension, each one of us) had received an upgrade, being elevated from servants to friends. Friends know each other. They know what they can ask for.

We have also been upgraded beyond friendship and have been called children of God—sons and daughters of the Most High (see 1 John 3:1; Rom. 8:14-17). Living as God's *children* gives us confidence that we can access Heaven whenever we want to, and that we can obtain whatever we want and need. We also become increasingly cognizant of the authority that we have as royal sons and daughters to release to the rest of the earth what we have received in the Kingdom of God.

We are able to enjoy an ever-deeper sense of intimacy, which in turn releases a greater measure of confidence for releasing the benefits of Kingdom authority. From within this place of intimacy, I understand that it is the Father's good pleasure to give me the Kingdom (see Luke 12:32). Healing, which is a revelation of His Name and, therefore, of the will of God and His Kingdom, can be released in and through me. In other words, as a son, I am a carrier of His glory, through the intimate relationship I have with Him.

To bring this back to treasure hunting: When I'm on a treasure hunt, I simply release whatever I have accessed in His presence.

Learning to live as a son has helped me grow in confidence as I encounter those who need a miracle in their bodies. I have learned that I have what it takes to broker God's Kingdom, because I am a son and I know it. I have heard the words for myself: "This is my son…." As a result, I have become more convinced that the Father has specifically given me the keys to the Kingdom and has commissioned me to transact Kingdom business on His behalf (see Matt. 16:19). Healing, therefore, is based less on a certain gifting that I might possess than it is on my assuming my role as a Kingdom son and businessman in the family business.

Christ in You, the Hope of Glory

Jesus Christ also lives *in* me in order to live *through* me. Paul put it this way: "Christ in you, the hope of glory" (Col. 1:27). Because He is in me, I have what it takes to reveal the glory of God through my life. Jesus said, "The kingdom of God is within you" (see Luke 17:21). God is always looking for those who will release what is inside of them.

I cannot save anyone, but Christ in me can save everyone. I cannot deliver anyone, but Christ in me can deliver everyone. Similarly, I cannot heal anyone, but Christ in me can heal everyone. Giving the Kingdom away is simply giving away the Jesus inside of us.

Of course, in one sense, I have as much of Christ as I will ever get, but in another sense, there is still more of Him being formed in me (see Gal. 4:19). And the more Christ is formed in me, the more I will have to give away. Do you see how the ministry of healing is simply releasing the presence of Christ that is residing within you?

Let's Talk About It

Which member of the Trinity do you tend to address most often in your prayers? Talk about possible reasons for your answer. Over the years, how have your prayers changed as your relationship with God deepened? What evidence can you share regarding your growing awareness of your sonship or daughterhood?

My breakthrough in understanding this principle came in January 2001. We had a young man living with us at the time who had been disabled for three months because he had ruptured a disk in his lower back while at work. He had just gone through surgery, but that had not helped him. He was bedridden and in constant pain. I felt horrible, watching him suffer so much pain without being able to help him.

I believed in healing, but I did not believe I had the ability to minister God's healing power. Twenty-three years prior, a woman died an hour after I prayed for her, and I truly believed that I had killed her because I did not have enough faith and was not gifted. So, for twenty-three years I did not pray over anyone for healing. I jokingly told those who asked for prayer that at best they would stay the same, but they could get worse or die.

One night as we were preparing for a fellowship group in our home, this young man asked for a few of the guys from the group to help him out to the couch where he could lie down to participate with us and take his mind off the pain. However, he couldn't help writhing with pain throughout the meeting, and eventually he became the focus of the meeting. Finally, he pleaded with me to pray for God to heal him.

Reluctantly, I succumbed to his desperate plea. I figured his condition could not get any worse, and besides, with no one else in the room who had the gift of healing, I was the best option available. I instructed the guys who had brought him out to the couch to stand him up. I went to him and hesitantly placed my hand on his back.

I was just about to launch into a comforting prayer to help him in his suffering, but before I could, he yelled out, "Do you feel the fire on my back where your hand is?" To my amazement, my hand felt like it was on fire, and I had not even prayed!

A few moments later, he bent over, and then jumped high in the air and exclaimed, "This is amazing! All of the pain is gone; I am healed!" He continued, "This is amazing…this is amazing…!" and then he started crying as he continued to jump around our living room demonstrating his complete healing. At one point, he sat down on the couch, looked up at me with tears of joy, and then jumped off the couch into a flying karate kick.

I was shocked. First, because he was healed as I had placed my hand on his back, and second, because my hand was still on fire, even though it was no longer on his back. Realizing that this was a "God thing," I asked if anyone else needed to be healed. Two others immediately responded, and as I placed my hand on them, they too were instantaneously healed.

This is how I came to understand that healing is not necessarily about gifting, but rather the released manifest presence of God. Christ in *me*, the hope of glory.

I often travel to churches, activating them in supernatural divine healing. One of the common misconceptions I encounter is that healing is a matter of learning all of the techniques and formulas to increase effectiveness. They often expect me to offer them a ten-point "how to" on getting people healed. While principles can facilitate breakthrough, I have found that physical healing is much more a matter of simply releasing His presence.

Often I will use a technique that brought healing breakthrough in the past, only to find it completely ineffective, even when all of the factors are exactly the same as before. So I repeat: The common denominator to getting people healed is His glorious presence released through risk.

Anointed Beyond Our Ability

I suppose many believers are intimidated by the idea of ministering supernaturally because they just do not feel that they have the necessary ability to release the Kingdom with confidence.

Unfortunately, too many of them are unaware that they have been actually anointed *beyond* their ability. I believe that every believer has the potential to operate in the supernatural, that every believer has the potential ability to heal the sick, prophesy, and set people free.

I base my belief on Jesus' statement in John 17:18 as He was praying for the disciples. He said to the Father, "As you sent me into the world, I have sent them into the world." Similarly, after the resurrection, Jesus informed the disciples: "As the Father has sent me, I am sending you" (John 20:21).

There are two questions that we must ask in order to understand the significance of Jesus' commission to the disciples. The first is, "Why was He sent?" and then the second is, "How was He sent?" The answer to these two questions will give us the insight we need into why and how we are to be sent ourselves.

Why was He sent? In Jesus' first recorded sermon, He stated, "He has sent me to proclaim freedom for the prisoners and recovery of sight for the blind, to set the oppressed free, to proclaim the year of the Lord's favor" (Luke 4:18b-19). Jesus had been sent to accomplish these four specific things, which are the fulfillment of the Messianic mission found in Isaiah 61:1-7.

Because Jesus said, "As the Father has sent me, I am sending you," we-you and I-have therefore been *sent* to do the same things Jesus did. We too have been *sent* to proclaim freedom for the prisoners and recovery of sight for the blind, to release the oppressed, and to proclaim the year of the Lord's favor. This means that we are supposed to be releasing the Kingdom wherever we go, to whomever we meet. That was His mission, and it has become our mission as well.

Next, we need to know *how* Jesus accomplished His mission, because from my perspective that mission seems totally impossible. For the answer, we must turn back to Jesus' first sermon, recorded in the fourth chapter of Luke. Quoting from Isaiah 61:1, Jesus announced that "The Spirit of the Sovereign Lord is on me, because the Lord has anointed me...." Hence, the way Jesus was able to fulfill the mission His Father had given Him was that the Holy Spirit anointed Him. You could say that He Himself was anointed beyond His ability.

In his sermon at Cornelius' house, Peter explained that "God anointed Jesus of Nazareth with the Holy Spirit and power," and that "he went around doing good and healing all who were under the power of the devil, because God was with him" (Acts 10:38). Jesus was called to an impossible mission that could only have been accomplished by being anointed with the Holy Spirit. How much more then must we too be anointed with the Holy Spirit in order to function beyond our natural ability.

The word for *anointed* in the Hebrew language is the word *messhiach*, from which we get the English word "Messiah," which means "Anointed One." The Greek counterpart to *messhiach* is *christos*, from which we get the English word "Christ." The term "Christian" is the Greek word *christianos,* or "anointed ones," and is from the same root as *christos,* which is *chrio* (to anoint).

Jesus told them, "If you forgive anyone's sins, their sins are forgiven; if you do not forgive them, they are not forgiven" (John 20:23). Notice that Jesus was giving the disciples authority to do what they could not have done on their own. Only God can forgive sins, which is why the religious leaders accused Jesus of blasphemy. Yet Jesus was able to forgive sins because He was anointed, and with that anointing came the authority to do only what God could do.

Along with the disciples' anointing came the authority to do what they had been commissioned to do. He was basically saying that whatever they decided to do, He would back them up.

Let's Talk About It

Why can we say that God's anointing is for everybody, regardless of his or her personalities, gifts, and personal history? Talk about times you have stopped short of operating in the anointing, settling instead for the limits of your own strength. How can you muster the courage to take new risks of faith?

It is just as easy to heal people as it is to forgive their sins (that was the point of the story about the paralytic in Luke 5:17-26). Both healing and forgiving sins require authority from God. By the same token, when Jesus announced that the disciples had authority to forgive sins, He was also implying that they had authority to heal the sick, prophesy, and set people free from demonic strongholds. The "if" simply meant that it was up to the disciples to do it.

Jesus was sent with a mission to destroy the works of the devil and usher in the blessings of Heaven. We have been sent with the same mission: "As the Father has sent me, I am sending you." Jesus could not have done the mission without an impartation of anointing through the Holy Spirit. He used His authority to bring Heaven to earth.

Treasure hunters are simply those who understand the anointing they have received through the Holy Spirit. They utilize the authority they have been entrusted with to destroy the works of the devil and release the blessings of God. Treasure hunters live naturally supernatural lifestyles, and they have found a way to allow the overflow of their lives to bring Heaven to earth—even in the mini-mart!

Let's Receive It

I release an encounter in which you hear your heavenly Father say, "You are My daughter/son." I see new levels of confidence in declaring, "Your Kingdom come, your will be done." I declare that you have what it takes to be a treasure hunter that changes the world wherever you are.

Let's Do It!

1.) Begin to declare God's will over specific things in your life that need His intervention. Release His presence and power through the words you proclaim.

2.) Utilize your status of sonship or daughterhood throughout the week. Journal the breakthroughs you get and report back to the group next week.

FIVE

The Naturally Supernatural Lifestyle: Relaxing Releases More Revival

I used to live in Huntington Beach, California, where I loved to body surf and body board. When I was first learning how to ride waves, I went out to body surf on a small-four-foot-wave day without any fins on my feet to help me catch the waves. I was having a lot of fun being thrown over the "falls" and crashing around in the churning whitewater. The water was only about shoulder high after each wave rolled through, so there seemed to be no imminent danger of drowning.

Then, without any warning, a rogue set of waves came rolling in. They looked like mountainous cliffs as they surged toward me. My first instinct was to run, but I couldn't since I was in the water. I started swimming madly toward the shore. The current, however, kept pulling me out toward the oncoming gargantuan waves. I realized that it was useless to try to escape them.

Turning around toward the ocean, I began to swim for all I was worth in an attempt to get over the first wave, which was probably about ten feet high. (When you are on your stomach, ten feet looks like twenty!) About halfway up the face of the wave, I realized I was not going to make it.

The powerful wave pitched me backward and I landed upside-down in the water. Immediately, I was in "the spin cycle" and did not know which way was up. Furthermore, the impact of hitting the water with such force took most of my breath away. I panicked.

It was relentless. Just as I would almost make it to the surface, the power of the wave would suck me back into the depths. It seemed like some invisible force was determined to make me submit as it held me under the water. Full of terror, I continued to struggle with every ounce of energy I could muster.

Breathless, I finally struggled to the surface, coughing up salt water and gasping for air. As I looked up, I could not believe my eyes; another wave, larger than the first one, was coming fast upon me. I was now trapped in the impact zone, and before I could get a full breath of air, the next mountain crashed onto me, sending me somersaulting to the bottom of the ocean, which was now about ten feet down.

I felt like a rag doll being shaken underneath the water. Once again, I came up gasping for air and coughing up the sea that had filled my lungs, only to face a third wave, larger than the previous ones, which pummeled me without mercy. This time, I could feel every cell in my body crying out for oxygen, and I knew that I was going to die.

In that moment, I remembered someone telling me that the best way to get back to the surface was by relaxing. Underwater and in such a perilous situation, however, it sure didn't seem very natural just to rest. But I no longer had enough strength to fight my way to the surface, so I decided to relax and accept the consequences. Oddly enough, as soon as I relaxed, I could feel myself rising toward the surface. I popped up and took two or three big breaths before the set wave (the largest of the set) came crashing down on me, throwing me into the spin cycle one more time.

This time, instead of struggling for the surface, I simply rested, knowing that the air inside of my lungs would float me to freedom. Sure enough, in just a few seconds I was at the surface once again. Thoroughly exhausted from my near-death experience. I finally made it back to shore, where I lay on the sand like a beached whale, coughing up salt water.

I have been in similar waves since, and while they are still intimidating, I have learned to relax, even though I am sometimes tempted to fight my way through them. I have come to realize that my best effort is no match for the power of the sea.

I often feel the same way when someone approaches me with an overwhelming physical disability that needs to be healed. In my desire to facilitate his or her seemingly impossible miracle breakthrough, I am often tempted to work harder than I should. I must remind myself to relax and let God's supernatural Kingdom power work through me naturally.

Let's Talk About It

See if each of you can come up with a true story of a time when relaxing your effort was the best way to success. It doesn't have to be a prayer story to illustrate the principle. After you have come up with some illustrations, see if you can put the principle into words.

Performance Treadmill

As Christians we can all too easily get caught up in religious performance and strive for God's acceptance, working in our own strength to demonstrate the Kingdom of God with signs and wonders, miracles, healing, and prophetic words. Usually, all we end up demonstrating is performance anxiety, which results in spiritual, emotional, and physical exhaustion.

Working and striving in the Kingdom may give us temporary fulfillment, but the best thing we can do is to rest in what Jesus has already provided for us. Jesus gave this invitation:

> *Come to me, all you who are weary and burdened, and I will give you rest. Take my yoke upon you and learn from me, for I am gentle and humble in heart, and you will find rest for your souls. For my yoke is easy and my burden is light* (Matthew 11:28-30).

Jesus was speaking to those who had exhausted themselves in their religious efforts to experience true spiritual life. His context for this invitation was His description of the miracles that took place in the various cities He had visited (see Matt. 11:20-24), where, despite these miracles, the religious leaders had rejected the revelation of truth, content to rely upon their religious performance and good works to gain God's approval.

Jesus implies that they will never find true approval, despite all of their religious efforts. The harder religious ones try, the less effective they are in their spirituality. On the other hand, little children can easily see their need for Jesus. He has extended His invitation to everyone, but only those who humble themselves like a child will be able to access it.

When we operate out of a deep-down knowledge of our acceptance and approval in Christ, based upon the work that He completed on the cross, we can relax in God's presence. There is no need for performance. No longer does our striving have to consume our energy. We can naturally rest in His supernatural presence.

"By Sunday morning, you will have a testimony"

Whenever I speak somewhere, I try to bring some students from our School of Supernatural Ministry. I love to include them during the meetings. Often I will invite them on the stage to give prophetic words and words of knowledge pertaining to physical ailments of people in the audience.

On one occasion, I was assigning specific time slots for various students to share testimonies of how God had used them to heal people in and outside of the church. When I came to Joe, he turned white with fear when I chose him to give a testimony. He sheepishly explained that, while he had been in the school for a year, he had never actually prayed for someone who had been healed, although he had seen others do it.

I told him not to worry: "By Sunday morning, you will have a testimony." And I put his name down. His face turned five shades whiter. I encouraged him to relax and just release what was already inside of him, assuring him that he would participate in someone's healing before Sunday morning.

On Saturday night, I invited all of the students to the stage to give words of knowledge, and then I had them go out to the audience to pray for those with the ailments they had identified. Joe had the impression that God wanted to heal someone's knee. About twenty minutes into the prayer time, Joe started jumping up and down, along with the person he had been praying for. "He's healed! He's healed!" Joe shouted over and over.

I brought them to the stage, where the man shared how he had severed his ACL ligament sixteen years prior and could not bend his knee, let alone put weight on it while bending it. On cue, he began doing deep knee bends, jumping up and down, and running and dancing around the auditorium. The crowd went wild because they all knew him quite well and were aware of his previous debilitation.

On Sunday morning, Joe shared with the congregation how he had felt besieged with anxiety at the thought of giving a testimony about healing when he had not yet seen anyone healed. He went on to share about the night before, how, as he began to interview the man with the "knee problem," he was even more uptight when he discovered that this man needed not only healing, but more—he needed a creative miracle. Joe told how he had redoubled his efforts, utilizing every principle he had ever been taught related to healing. Nothing had worked. Finally, out of utter frustration, he said, "I'm just going to do what Kevin does: I'm just going to relax and release the Father's presence."

With a huge smile, he reported that as soon as he stopped striving and simply rested in God's presence, a feeling of fire came on the man's leg, and he was instantly healed! Joe is no longer one of those people who is intimidated about praying for healing—even radical healing—because now he has discovered the Kingdom key of resting in God's presence.

This is true for anybody. The more we strive to release the Kingdom, the less effective our efforts become. Less is more when it comes to unlocking Heaven and living a naturally supernatural life.

Let's Talk About It

Practically speaking, how can you relax in overwhelming circumstances and needs in order to better release the Kingdom? Share with each other what you have learned about this principle.

_____

_____

_____

_____

_____

_____

_____

_____

_____

_____

_____

_____

_____

_____

_____

_____

_____

_____

_____

_____

_____

_____

_____

_____

Jesus Worked So That We Don't Have To

On the seventh day, after God had finished all of the work of Creation, He rested. Interestingly, there is no mention of a night and day (see Gen. 2:2-3), the implication being that God continued to rest once He had completed the work He had intended. Moreover, nowhere in Scripture are we told that God went back to tinker with Creation once He entered into rest. Once He was done, He was done.

On the cross, Jesus declared, "It is finished" (John 19:30). What was finished? He had fulfilled everything required for purchasing our salvation. He had accomplished everything the Father had given Him to do to restore our rightful inheritance in the Kingdom. Jesus had done all that so that we could rest along with Him and His Father. He had provided a way for us to take a permanent spiritual vacation from all religious striving and performance. No more work would ever be required. Jesus worked so that we don't have to!

God is making us new in Christ; as a result, He has invited each of us into spiritual rest. No more work is required; no additions are necessary; we are simply invited to rest as new creations.

How does this fit with Jesus' declaration that He and His Father are always working (see John 5:17)? There is no account of Jesus ever taking a vacation. He is still working today. When you pray, you will never get a recorded message saying: "God is on vacation and will not be able to work a miracle until He gets back in two weeks. Until then, just hang in there and work it out yourself." We have to realize that, even as He works, Jesus is always resting. He does not need a vacation because He continually works from a place of rest. God's supernatural intervention comes to us as the natural overflow of who He is—His nature.

In Matthew 9:37-38, Jesus looks for those who will work in the harvest fields. The apostle Paul encourages us to respect all of those who work hard (see 1 Thess. 5:12), exhorting, "Whatever you do, work at it with all your heart …" (Col. 3:23). In fact, if we do not work, the Kingdom cannot be released to those around us. However, the only effective work is that which arises from a place of divine rest. We are no longer working *for* approval, but rather *from* approval. As we learn to work in rest, we begin to be effective in living a naturally supernatural life.

Fruitfulness Flows from Rest

Jesus stated, "I am the vine; you are the branches. If you remain in me and I in you, you will bear much fruit; apart from me you can do nothing" (John 15:5). Fruitfulness flows out of restful abiding. Only those who remain (rest) in Him will bear Kingdom fruit. Remaining in Him means resting in the work that He has provided for us, as well as resting in His presence.

Developing the character of Christ and releasing the Kingdom of Christ should be a natural outgrowth of the rest that we experience as we remain in Him. As we rest in His presence, soaking in the nutrients of His love and grace, we become capable of producing Kingdom fruit.

Let's Talk About It

What do you think working out of rest looks like? Share an example from your own life about how you accomplished more with less effort. What prevents you from resting? What are some ways in which you can sustain a lifestyle of rest?

Think about it: what does an apple seed do to produce fruit? Does it strive and struggle to produce a sapling? Does the tree trunk grimace as is pushes out the limbs and leaves, as if they will not develop without effort? Do the limbs muster up every ounce of performance to produce the fruit?

The effort should be naturally supernatural. Striving to produce Kingdom fruit by means of the effort of our own performance results in artificial fruit. What good is that? Artificial fruit is like religion. God told Adam to be fruitful and increase, not to strive and increase (see Gen. 1:28). The only authentic fruitfulness in the Kingdom of God grows out of rest.

In the Garden of Eden, the man and the woman were supposed to eat of the tree of life (a symbol of Jesus, the vine, as described in John 15), which denoted the presence of God. Only by means of this fellowship and communion could Adam and Eve enjoy naturally supernatural fruitfulness. When they decided to eat of the tree of the knowledge of good and evil, however, their effort to be like God and attempt to attain wisdom apart from God led to religious performance, artificial fruit, and a sentence of death.

Thanks to Jesus, the "second Adam" (see 1 Cor. 15:45-48), we can turn it around. Once again, we can eat daily from the tree of life, Jesus, the True Vine; He provides the supernatural nutrients to produce supernatural fruit. Once again, the Kingdom of God can be released to the world. It happens only through resting in Him.

Peter is a great example of someone who operated in the supernatural out of rest. Peter was not even trying to heal people when he walked past them and his shadow fell on them (see Acts 5:15)! He was just continually resting in God's presence, being a habitation of His presence, effortlessly leaking what was inside of him. This is the natural outflow of God's rest. Remaining in the presence of Jesus naturally produces supernatural Kingdom fruit.

On several occasions, I have just put my hand on someone's shoulder, arm, or back while saying hello, only to find out that, as I touched that person, he or she was completely healed. I call these "drive-by healings." They happen apart from any personal effort to release God's Kingdom; they are simply a result of living in revival rest.

After one Sunday evening service at Bethel Church, a sixty-year-old woman approached me for healing prayer. This woman experienced chronic pain throughout her entire body and never seemed to get breakthrough, despite the fact that she had received prayer from everyone on our team several times.

I was exhausted from a full day's ministry, and I just wanted to go home, so I tactfully directed her to one of our Bethel School of Supernatural Ministry students, explaining that the student could heal her just as easily as I could. The woman, however, pleaded with me to pray for her one last time before going home. Irritated, I reached out my hand toward her forehead and shouted out, "Well, then, be healed. I release a twenty-year-old body to you in Jesus' name."

At that, she threw her head back, let out an ecstatic yell, and fell straight backward onto the floor with a crack. I was concerned that she may have injured herself, but when she finally stood back up, she said that all of the pain had left her body—she was healed!

Further, she explained that someone else had prophesied those very words just a few minutes before I had declared them over her. She went on to say that when she heard the words for the second time, the presence of God came flooding into her, filling her entire body with healing ecstasy, and she could not stand under it. She stood there in utter shock, completely healed.

Even though I had been irritated and reluctant, and I had had no faith for this woman's healing, my decision to speak the words released the Kingdom in her body. She received a breakthrough because I chose to partner with God to release His presence.

The more we cultivate our relationship with the true vine, the tree of life, and rest in His presence, the more we will naturally find ourselves releasing the Kingdom to those around us. That's the way to live—pursuing a naturally supernatural life by operating out of a place of true rest.

Healing Is a Normal Expression of the Kingdom

When He first sent the twelve disciples out, Jesus said, "As you go, proclaim this message: 'The kingdom of heaven has come near.' Heal the sick…" (Matt. 10:7-8). Healing was intended to be an integral part of demonstrating that the Kingdom of God is near. Therefore, healing is an essential tool for the treasure hunter, who is attempting to convince someone to believe the message.

Healing is a normal expression of the Kingdom of God. Throughout Scripture, we can read promises and testimonies about this. See, for example, Exodus 15:26, Isaiah 53:4-5, and Matthew 4:23. Jesus sent out His disciples to demonstrate the Kingdom just as He had done—through healings, miracles, and signs and wonders (see John 20:21). Did they do it? The Book of Acts tells their treasure-hunting stories!

Let's Talk About It

Create some "what if" scenarios, either using scriptural accounts or modern-day testimonies of how miracles were instrumental in convincing people of the truth of Christ. What if no healing or miracle had occurred? Would unbelievers have been convinced that a loving God is alive and worth turning to? On the other hand, what if an unmistakable supernatural component had been introduced into a situation? What might have transpired? Why is supernatural healing so important in communicating the Good News?

_____

_____

_____

_____

_____

_____

_____

_____

_____

_____

_____

_____

_____

_____

_____

_____

_____

_____

_____

Inhale, Exhale

People don't have to remind themselves to breathe. All of us take in a breath and then let it out naturally. We were designed to inhale and exhale without thinking about it. In fact, if we do not exhale what we have inhaled, we will die. What started out as life, if it is not given away, will result in death.

Similarly, it should be natural for us to inhale God's presence and then to exhale His presence on those around us who need His miraculous power. Renewal is breathing in. Revival is breathing out. We need both to live a naturally supernatural life.

Once I had a vision of inhaling the names of God as they came to me one by one from the mouth of Jesus (represented as a Lion) and then, just as naturally as I had received the breath into my lungs, I exhaled and gave it away. As the vision continued, I saw a great multitude of people with mouths wide open, gasping for air. As I breathed out what I had inhaled—the names of God—I saw those very names coming out of my mouth in slow motion and magnified to those in the crowd.

I saw joy go into one person's mouth, and immediately she began to dance and laugh with fullness of joy. Peace entered another person's mouth. Wisdom, counsel, abundance, acceptance, healing, deliverance, salvation—whatever the person needed, the breath brought the very characteristic of God's name that would meet his or her need and desire. This is bringing Heaven to earth. This is living a naturally supernatural life. When God breathes His supernatural breath on us—and then through us—anything is possible.

Unfortunately, most Christians stop by inhaling what they need from God's presence and then stingily keeping all of it to themselves, thus causing renewal to fall short of God's end purpose—revival. He always intends for us to breathe out what we have breathed in.

We need the breath of God in order to live the supernatural life that we have been called to. We need the living Word of God speaking life into our circumstances, needs, and destiny. We need the life-giving breath of God to empower those words to work their full effect. We have been called to represent the Kingdom of God on earth, which can sometimes feel impossible to accomplish. For me, I know that I need more of His breath every day if I expect to live in my destiny as a revivalist and world-changer. We can only exhale what we have inhaled from His presence.

Sometimes, I will release an impartation of the breath of the lion of Judah, breathing on people as a prophetic act to release what they need from His presence. I remember one woman who had had fibromyalgia for fifteen years. She was in such constant pain that she could barely function during the day or sleep through the night. After receiving the impartation of the lion's breath, she began to notice that the pain throughout her body was decreasing, and she felt energy flowing into her limbs.

She came back the next day and reported that she had actually overslept. She had slept through the entire night without waking once, and she had not taken her usual dose of pain medication and sleep aids. She also reported that when she woke up that morning, she had immediately gotten out of bed and began doing household chores. As she completed her morning's work, she suddenly realized that it usually took her two hours to just start moving around because of stiffness and pain. She had been completely healed as the breath of God blew on her the night before through my breath!

I have heard reports of people receiving freedom from fears, release into joy, wisdom for a decision, comfort, encouragement, and so on as I have released the breath of God onto them.

This is just one more way of talking about living a naturally supernatural life. God has an inexhaustible abundance of life that He wants to pour through us, if only we will allow Him to continually breathe on us.

Let's Talk About It

Talk about an experience, firsthand or otherwise, in which God's supernatural power came into a situation without apparent effort on anybody's part. What did you learn from the experience? How did you make use of what you learned?

_____

_____

_____

_____

_____

_____

_____

_____

_____

_____

_____

_____

_____

_____

_____

_____

_____

_____

_____

_____

If We Open Our Eyes, He Will Open Their Eyes

God told my son Chad that He was going to teach him how to pray. As he was reading Matthew 6:9-10, he could not get past the phrase, "Our Father, in heaven," reading it over several times.

As he contemplated these verses, God asked him to describe what came to mind when he heard the phrase, "Our Father." Chad replied, "Your children, the Church." God responded, "That's not big enough; you have to think bigger. You have to think about your city and the world." God went on to say that He was going to give Chad a sign that day, and that He was going to teach him how to help release a great wave of evangelism.

After praying, Chad went about his day looking for the sign. Nothing seemed to stand out as the sign until that afternoon when he saw a woman wearing a knee brace, who was driving a motorized cart in the grocery store. He approached the woman to inquire about the apparent injury and found out that she had recently fallen off some stairs and torn the ligaments in her knee. She also had severe neck pain from the accident.

He asked her if he could pray for her. She said that she was a Hindu and did not believe in his God, but that he could go ahead and pray. So, right in the middle of aisle 12 of a local supermarket, he laid his hand on her shoulder and released the presence of Christ.

After the short prayer, she reported that she felt fire in her back and that all the pain had left immediately. He asked about her knee and she said she couldn't tell without taking off the knee brace, which she did. She began pacing up and down the aisle without any pain or limp. Coming back to Chad, she said to him, "I want the same Jesus you have," and she received Jesus into her heart.

Chad went off to pay for his groceries. As he was standing in the checkout line, he heard an announcement over the intercom instructing one of the employees to go to aisle 12 to retrieve an abandoned motorized cart. Marveling at the miraculous sign that had just occurred, he heard the Lord say, "That is not the sign."

A little confused, he made his way back to his car. En route, he noticed a man with a patch covering his right eye. Instantly, the Lord spoke to him and said, "This is the sign I am giving you today." Chad stopped the man to ask him why he had a patch over his eye and found out that he was completely blind in that eye. As Chad placed his hand over the patched eye, the man felt an immediate change. He then removed the patch to discover that his blind eye had been completely healed.

At that moment, the Lord spoke again to my son and said, "This is what I will do if the Church will purpose to be the light of the world; I will open up the eyes of the unsaved." In other words, if we will open our eyes, then He will open their eyes.

In Second Corinthians 4:4, Paul pointed out "the god of this age has blinded the minds of unbelievers, so that they cannot see the light of the gospel that displays the glory of Christ, who is the image of God." The sign Chad received was not so much about healing someone's eye as it was about blindness. Certainly, the healing of this man's blind eye was amazing, but miracles themselves are signs pointing to Christ. God wants to heal eyes, but more than that, He wants to open people's spiritual eyes to see the Kingdom.

In Luke 10:17-20, the disciples were excited about the amazing, miraculous breakthroughs they had experienced, while Jesus' focus was never deflected from the eternal consequences: "Rejoice that your names are written in heaven." The ultimate goal for any supernatural encounter is to establish or increase relationship with God.

The question is whether or not we will be willing to open our eyes to the blind around us. Will we take ownership for the world that God has placed in our sphere of influence?

Declarations Make a Difference

Jesus taught us to pray, "Your kingdom come, your will be done, on earth as it is in heaven" (Matt. 6:10). Unfortunately, many incorrectly quote this verse, adding "may" or "let" to the beginning: "[May] Your kingdom come, [let] Your will be done," which turns it into a hopeful prayer rather than a declaration as He intended it. Nothing in the Greek text warrants this sense of pleading for His Kingdom to come or hoping that He will somehow grant our request!

The problem with praying from this perspective is that it wrongfully relinquishes all of our responsibility for the outcome of breakthrough, placing it all on God and His supposed, predetermined will. No wonder God gets a bad rap when things do not work out in people's lives the way they had hoped. We are relying on God to do what He is relying on us to do!

Besides, the mood of the verb "come" is declarative in Greek. In other words, Jesus wanted us to *declare* His Kingdom—"Your Kingdom come right now." This declaration springs from the authority that we carry as royal sons and daughters (as discussed last week). Jesus was teaching His disciples that they carried a responsibility to release the Kingdom. As authorized representatives, they must determine where and when it needs to come.

Moreover, Greek verbs have not only moods but also tenses (when an action takes place) and senses (how the action happens—how it is completed). When Jesus taught His disciples to pray "come," He used the aorist verb tense/sense, which normally connotes a past tense and punctiliar sense (meaning a one-time occurrence). However, when the aorist tense/sense is used in combination with the declarative mood, as is the case in this verse, the verb tense changes from past to present, while the sense remains punctiliar, meaning a one-time occurrence.

In other words, Jesus was teaching that we would have to release the Kingdom every time that we need to unlock Heaven and bring it to earth. Unlocking Heaven is not just a one-time prayer event that releases continual breakthrough for the rest of our lives or a futuristic prayer regarding the return of Christ. It is an ongoing, daily lifestyle of declaring His Kingdom, bringing it in wherever and whenever it is needed.

Sadly, some people approach Kingdom breakthrough like the man who continually asked God for a job. Every day, he complained that God was not keeping His promise to provide for his every need. Finally, God said to the man, "Hey, I would like to provide you with a job, but it sure would help if you went to an interview!"

We are mistaken when we believe that it is God's full responsibility to bring breakthrough in our circumstances. The release of the Kingdom is contingent upon our decision to "go to the interview." We must be willing to partner with God for breakthrough.

As members of the royal priesthood (see 1 Pet. 2:9), we have been given a responsibility to declare, "Your Kingdom come." As priests of God, we are to declare His rule—His influence—wherever we see injustice; we are to mediate Heaven to earth and into every situation that needs God's intervention.

It is important for us to realize that when we do declare the coming of His Kingdom, we are actually releasing Heaven to earth with our words. The Bible tells us that we have the power of life and death in our tongues (see Prov. 18:21; James 3:3-12). The reason Jesus warned us that we would be judged according to the words we speak (see Matt. 12:36-37) is that our words make a difference in people's lives and circumstances—our words can either curse or release the Kingdom to bring blessing.

Let's Talk About It

Have you sometimes neutralized your prayers by failing to pray out of full confidence that God would come and act (essentially saying, "may your Kingdom come—please, if it be Your will")? Talk about how you can develop the habit of *declaring* the coming of the Kingdom of God. How can you be sure that your declarations match up with God's will?

Sowing Seed

In the parable of the seed and the sower in Matthew chapter 13, only twenty-five percent of the seed actually produced fruit. The seed, however, was sown without discrimination into each type of soil. Of course the Father wants all the seed that He sows to become fruitful, but apparently the fact that some of it fails to become fruitful does not prevent Him from sowing. In the same way, we have to trust that the seed of the message of the Kingdom will find receptive hearts and what has been sown will be cultivated to maturity.

Paul wrote: "I planted the seed, Apollos watered it, but God has been making it grow" (1 Cor. 3:6). While our goal is to see people established in the Kingdom, our job is simply to do whatever task may be required in the process. Sometimes Paul planted, while at other times he watered what someone else had planted. Regardless, God used him to bring Kingdom growth to the seeds. He didn't have to worry about how it would happen.

A perfect example of this is Philip's experience with the Ethiopian eunuch (see Acts 8). This was an amazing treasure hunt, in which Philip obeyed the guidance of the Holy Spirit and the man was saved. Interestingly, after Philip had baptized him, we read, "When they came up out of the water, the Spirit of the Lord suddenly took Philip away, and the eunuch did not see him again, but went on his way rejoicing" (Acts 8:39).

Wait a minute. He did not have time to get him into a local church. What was the Holy Spirit thinking? Why did He not allow Philip to stay with him long enough to get "added" to the Church? Could it be that God trusted that what had been sown would produce the fruit that was intended? Historical accounts from early Church Fathers of the faith such as Irenaeus (AD 130–202) indicate that this eunuch went back to Ethiopia and was very influential in establishing the Gospel in Ethiopia as well as other parts of northern Africa.

Most of the time, we will be unaware of the underlying strategies by which God is directing a person's life. At some point we have to have confidence that "he who began a good work in you will carry it on to completion" (Phil. 1:6).

After a treasure hunt, we often get reports of people who seemed to have received very little impact from an encounter, only to find out later that the seed we sowed actually took root and began to sprout up later.

Other times, we encounter people who are absolutely ready and eager to jump into the treasure chest, commit themselves to Christ, and follow Him through discipleship. Such people seem to be almost "accidental" treasure.

Here's an example: one of our treasure-hunt teams went out looking for clues, but after about an hour without finding even one clue, one of the students from our School of Supernatural Ministry noticed that all of the clues seemed to point to his unsaved brother who lived in another state. They decided to call him on the phone and they found that he fit the description of all of the clues on their treasure map.

The students began to prophesy to the young man on the other end of the phone, calling out his destiny and the promises of salvation through receiving Christ. As the prophetic words revealed the secrets of his heart, the young man was so touched that the next day he drove to the church, where he met his brother and the treasure-hunt team.

He gave his heart to the Lord, and all weekend long people prophesied to him and prayed with him. At the end of the weekend, he announced that he was finished with a life of drug addiction and depression. He enrolled in a discipleship school while he awaited his term of enrollment in the School of Supernatural Ministry at Bethel Church.

Once this young man jumped into the treasure chest, he was so transformed by his encounter with the living Gospel that he decided to get trained to become a treasure hunter himself. Surely this is Jesus' ultimate desire for those who come into the treasure chest.

Being a treasure hunter is about finding treasure. Sometimes, our job is to uncover the hidden treasure, confident that someone else will come along to pick them up and get them into the treasure chest, the Church. Whatever the case, our responsibility is to be witnesses to the ends of the earth, with the goal of making disciples of all nations, which includes every subculture and every person.

There are still plenty of treasures to be found. They are everywhere. The best way to find your way to them is to cultivate a naturally supernatural life and to work from rest.

 # Let's Receive It

I release a new level of revival rest over you and into you. I pray that you would hear the words that Jesus heard at His baptism, "With him I am well pleased"– that you would have complete confidence of His approval of you before you ever even attempt to take risk to release God's Kingdom. I pray that your vision will expand to better see those who are waiting for an encounter with God. I release you into a new level of risk in declaring God's purposes in seemingly insurmountable circumstances.

Let's Do It!

1.) Take some risk this week to release God's Kingdom to someone, and then share a testimony with the group about it. How did you reach out to someone this week who needed an encounter with God? How was he or she they able to encounter "our father?"

2.) Write down the instances in which you found yourself working for approval from God and man this week. How were you able to revert to revival rest? Or not?

SIX

Hanging on to Every Word: Hungering for the *Rhema* Releases Revival

My wife, Theresa, is an incredible treasure hunter. She was in prayer one morning when the Holy Spirit spoke to her about going to a certain local supermarket to find some treasure before coming to our weekly pastors' staff meeting. She was running a little late that morning but decided to follow the prompting she had received. She walked into the store with "produce" and "grief" as her only clues.

As she stood there in the produce section, she began to evaluate all of the potential treasure. After five minutes or so, feeling a little bewildered that no one seemed to fit the description, she noticed a woman standing by the corn. Motionless and looking blankly into space, she appeared distraught as she stood with her cart.

Theresa approached her and explained about the treasure hunt she was on. Because of the "grief" clue she had received, she went on to ask whether the woman was dealing with any grief issues. The woman broke into tears, explaining that she had just recently lost her husband to cancer, and then, just a few days prior, their dog had died. She had hardly slept since then, and had not eaten anything. Through her tears, she explained that even though she was severely depressed, she felt like she needed to go to the store. Once she got to the produce department, however, she had no idea why she was there.

After listening with empathy, Theresa offered to pray with her. The woman agreed, and Theresa began praying prophetic prayers of hope and comfort. After she finished, the woman looked up at her, wiped away the tears, and asked, "Are you an angel?"

The best treasure hunters are the ones who not only learn to hear the voice of the Lord in the secret place of prayer, but who obey the directions they get.

Developing Healthy Hearing

Hearing God's voice is essential for treasure hunting. We must know what God's voice sounds like (even though much of the time it is not audible to our physical ears) in order to follow His directions, know His will, and gain His wisdom.

Although having a good understanding of the Bible is essential for every believer, it is not enough. Simply knowing what the Bible says, or having a good grasp of theology, will not provide the kind of specific guidance we need for bringing the Kingdom of God to earth in our daily lives. We must learn to listen to every whisper from Heaven.

For many Christians, the idea of hearing from God is very foreign. These same Christians have no problem petitioning God, expecting Him to hear them. But they have considerable difficulty believing that they can hear what He says to them. For too many Christians, "hearing from God" has been reduced to getting an insight from the Bible. Others are scared by the thought of hearing from God, because of all the kooks who claim to hear Him, thus giving a bad reputation to the whole idea.

Hearing from God personally is a scriptural idea. A well-known example is Moses, who had his first conversation with God at the burning bush (see Exod. 3). Gideon gained confidence to take on the Midianites when he negotiated with God's angel and used a fleece for confirmation purposes (see Judges 6:11-40). Paul heard Jesus' voice on the road to Damascus (see Acts 9:4-6) and Peter heard it regarding the "clean and unclean" animals (see Acts 10).

God does not always speak audibly. Peter, for example, heard Him in the context of a vision. It was important for Peter to see the vision of unclean animals being offered to him as food; the central message consisted of wordless communication. The Holy Spirit uses many ways to communicate God's words to our spirits. He has been given to us to communicate the plans and desires of the Father. The Holy Spirit does this through visions, dreams, prophetic words, words of wisdom, and words of knowledge (see 1 Cor. 12). He speaks in full sentences and in truncated syllables. He uses gestures and circumstances to symbolize specific meanings. He is always being creative about how He speaks.

Let's Talk About It

How do you most often hear God? What part do the Scriptures play in it? Tell the others in the group about a time when God spoke to you in a new-to-you way and how you recognized that it was Him.

Second-Guessing Yourself

We are in good company when we doubt that what we think we hear is really from God. Even Jesus was tempted to doubt what He had just heard. He had barely started His public ministry when He was driven out into the wilderness to be tempted by the devil (see Matt. 4:1-11). At least twice during those forty days, the devil taunted Him by saying "*If you are the Son of God….*"

Now Jesus had just heard His Father's audible voice from Heaven. In the previous chapter, we read about His baptism, when His Father said these words: "This is my Son, whom I love; with him I am well pleased" (Matt. 3:17). Nothing could have been clearer. Jesus knew He was the Son of the Father. And yet along came the devil, trying to plant doubts about it. I believe the devil understood that if he could get Jesus to doubt His hearing—that He was indeed a son—it would debilitate Him and prevent Him from fulfilling His destiny. He was trying to plant the doubt, "Did you really hear God correctly?"

Jesus didn't fall for that doubting line, but we often do. Our earliest ancestors started us down that road when they fell for the devil's strategy; they doubted what the Father had clearly told them. As God instructed Adam about the Garden, He said: "You are free to eat from any tree in the garden; but you must not eat from the tree of the knowledge of good and evil, for when you eat from it you will certainly die" (Gen. 2:16-17).

Adam told Eve what God had said, and the devil decided to make her doubt it, asking her, "Did God really say, 'You must not eat from any tree in the garden'?" (Gen. 3:1b). In other words, "Are you sure Adam really heard God correctly?"

We know the rest. Adam and Eve were destined to exercise authority over the earth, managing what God had created (see Gen. 1:28). Instead, they disobeyed God because those subtle doubts took hold. Eve was deceived into doubting what God had clearly told them, and she and Adam decided to do the exact thing God had forbidden them to do.

"HeBrews Coffee"?

In preparation for a treasure hunt in Santa Rosa, California, one of our School of Supernatural Ministry students thought he heard, "HeBrews Coffee," which is the name of the coffee shop located in our church building in Redding, California. He discarded the thought as flippant and inconsequential because it was so unlikely that the clue would have any significance some 250 miles away from Redding.

Throughout the preparation time (about three minutes), I kept reminding the group to go "out of the box," pursuing seemingly senseless words of knowledge. "If you have a thought," I told them, "write it down, even if it seems impossible." The thought "HeBrews Coffee" kept coming to this student's mind, but each time he dismissed it as his own, unrelated thoughts.

As he was going out with his treasure-hunting team, he once again heard "HeBrews Coffee" in his mind. This time, to appease his conscience, he decided to write it in very small letters at the very bottom of the page, well below the other clues he had heard and written down.

Their treasure map directed them to a local park. This student noticed a man sitting on a bench. While he had no clues to direct him to this man, he decided to chat with him to build rapport in case God could use that.

Their conversation turned to spiritual inquiries. The man shared that he was not a Christian, but that if he were, the only church he would ever consider attending would be a church in Redding, California, called Bethel Church. He explained his reason—that particular church has a little coffee shop inside called "HeBrews Coffee," with some of the best coffee he had ever tasted!

At once, the student pulled out the treasure map to show the man that this was a divine appointment. The man was amazed at the clue and he was receptive to the Good News as the student began to share it.

For his part, the student left that encounter convinced that His thoughts are our thoughts (see 1 Cor. 2:16) more than he had realized before.

Let's Talk About It

Talk about times when you doubted that you were hearing God's voice. What made you waver? In the end, what helped you discern?

_____

_____

_____

_____

_____

Distinguishing God's Voice from the Others

The authority and confidence to release the Kingdom of God into the world is founded upon the ability of individual Christians to clearly hear the voice of God and to comprehend the significance of what He says. Moreover, the ability to hear God's voice determines the level of risk we are willing to take to accomplish God's will in and through our lives.

Unfortunately, too many voices vie for our attention. You know as well as I do how difficult it can be to discern God's voice from the rest of them. Most of the voices come from our own thoughts, which barrage our minds almost without ceasing. Our thoughts come from many different sources: the media, other people, the devil, and so forth.

The quest, then, is to determine God's voice from among all of the varying voices speaking to us. The young boy Samuel had to work through this process when the priest Eli helped him discern God's voice (see 1 Sam. 3:1-18.) It wasn't instantaneous; he really thought he was hearing Eli's voice at first, and he needed help to tell the difference. Eventually, though, Samuel learned to be so sensitive to God's voice that he became a trusted and honored prophet in Israel.

Jesus uses a figure of speech to describe the way believers are designed to hear from God:

...The sheep listen to his voice. He calls his own sheep by name and leads them out. When he has brought out all his own, he goes on ahead of them, and his sheep follow him because they know his voice (John 10:3-4).

In other words, we become sensitive to our Shepherd's voice because we have learned what it sounds like. We know Him. It isn't really a question of whether or not He is speaking. He is. It's a question of distinguishing His voice, which may be soft at times, from the rest of the clamor of voices.

Hungry for Hearing

We won't even try to learn how to hear God's voice if we aren't hungry to hear from Him. A passing desire to hear something won't do the trick. We must be ravenously hungry, even desperate to hear God's voice.

This is the way Solomon describes the bride's desire to hear her bridegroom's voice:

My dove in the clefts of the rock, in the hiding places on the mountainside, show me your face, let me hear your voice; for your voice is sweet, and your face is lovely (Song of Solomon 2:14).

She also cries out, "You who dwell in the gardens with friends in attendance, let me hear your voice!" (Song of Sol. 8:13). This is a cry of desperation; she must hear his voice. Thus, she is completely focused on hearing it.

In his book of Proverbs, Solomon observed, "The appetite of laborers works for them; their hunger drives them on" (Prov. 16:26). When we are hungry to hear God's voice, our craving drives us until we find what we are looking for.

The writer to the Hebrews promised, "He [God] rewards those who earnestly seek him" (Heb. 11:6). Another translation for the phrase "earnestly seek him" is to "crave Him." In the context of hearing God's voice, our hunger, our craving to hear, is rewarded when He speaks to us.

Jesus promised, "Blessed are those who hunger and thirst for righteousness, for they will be filled" (Matt. 5:6). He also assured us that if we ask, we *will* receive (see Matt. 7:7; Luke 11:9). David declares: "He satisfies the thirsty and fills the hungry with good things" (Ps. 107:9; see also Luke 1:53). Our hunger and thirst to hear God's voice actually draw Him to speak to us.

The key, then, is to stay hungry and thirsty. One way to do that is to put yourself into situations where you simply must hear Him. For example, at times I may announce to the people with me in a restaurant that I am going to get some words of knowledge for our server. When he or she starts walking toward our table, I can feel my desperation rising—and I do hear from God.

Once my wife and I were eating out and I told her I was going to do this. Sure enough, when our server returned to our table, I "heard" (like a very clear thought) "bronchial problem." As it turned out, she had intense allergies. Theresa and I prayed for her and immediately she felt better. Shocked, she explained that her lungs were completely open and that she could breathe normally for the first time in a long time. Excitedly, she also exclaimed that her headache, another symptom of the allergies, had also left.

As we were leaving, I noticed a couple sitting behind us. Once again, I told Theresa that I intended to minister to them. I had not yet heard a thing from the Lord about them, so I just stopped next to their table and opened my mouth. I said to the husband, "Excuse me, this might sound a little strange, but by any chance do you have any [and at that very moment I heard the words] back pain?"

Interestingly, I only heard the specific words as I stepped out into the place where I had to hear. The man responded, "How did you know that?" Still holding a forkful of spaghetti, he explained that he had been experiencing intense pain in his back throughout dinner. As I began to release the presence of Jesus on him, his pain completely left.

We went on to minister to his wife, as Theresa got words of knowledge about her sleep problem, and at the end we introduced both of them to the Jesus who had just touched them. When we left their table about ten minutes later, we felt like long-time friends—all because I had put myself into a position in which I *had* to hear from God.

 ## Let's Talk About It

How do you make yourself more open to hearing God? How do you stay hungry? Share a time in which you heard God say to do something out of your comfort zone and you obeyed.

Hanging on Every Word

It's not enough to pay attention in a general sort of way to what God might want to say. You have to treat each word like a jewel. You have to ingest and digest every word, in fulfillment of Jesus' statement: "Man shall not live on bread alone, but on every word that comes from the mouth of God" (Matt. 4:4). We'll never be able to experience the fullness of life without hearing the voice of God.

Interestingly, the Greek word translated "word" in that passage is not *graphe*, which means "writing." Jesus was not recommending that we live on every *graphe*, or written Word of God in Scripture, but rather on every *rhema*, which means "communication" or "conversation." That's why He says He wants us to live on every word that comes from the mouth of God. It must be God's intention for people to have ongoing communication with Him in the context of a relationship.

As Paul put it, "faith comes from hearing, and hearing by the word [*rhema*] of Christ" (Rom. 10:17 NASB). Our life-sustaining faith comes by means of the conversation we have with God in the communion of His presence. Moreover, part of our armor as Christians is "the sword of the Spirit, which is the word [*rhema*] of God" (Eph. 6:17). The way Jesus Himself defeated the enemy's temptations was to hang onto every word that His Father spoke. He could overcome His enemies because He had a continual conversation with His Father.

I'm not saying that we don't need the Bible—not at all. The Scriptures represent a vital aspect of God's conversation with human beings:

> *All Scripture is God-breathed and is useful for teaching, rebuking, correcting and training in righteousness, so that the servant of God may be thoroughly equipped for every good work* (2 Timothy 3:16-17).

The Scriptures, alive with His presence, help us hear what God wants to say to us every day. Scripture is not comprehensive of all that God is speaking, but God does not contradict what He has already said in Scripture. God cannot be fully contained within the confines of Scripture; there is more to God than what is revealed there. Therefore, we do not need a proof text for everything we hear from God, but the written Word will be able to confirm any *rhema* communication that we believe He is speaking. True life comes from a relationship with God, not from the confirmation of that relationship.

Over the years, I have met many people who have studied the Scriptures but do not have the life of God. People can read and hear the words of the Bible on a daily basis, yet miss having a relationship with Christ. Our new life can only grow through the nourishment of the fresh daily "manna" of the words God speaks to our hearts.

Some of those living words are words of knowledge that release His Kingdom into the lives of others. Some of what we hear will direct our steps to find the people God wants to touch. Some of what we hear will give us His perspective on what we see in front of us. We need those words, every one of them. God doesn't waste any words.

Let's Talk About It

How do you and God communicate? What do you do if the communication you are hearing is contradictory to the Scriptures? How do the Scriptures work together with visions, dreams, ideas and thoughts, and prophecies? Can God say things and give us ideas that are not found in the Scriptures? Why or why not?

Really *Hearing* What He Says

In reference to Jesus' description of how His sheep know His voice (see John 10:3-4), it is interesting to note that sheep are nearsighted, but they have an overdeveloped sense of hearing that enables them to distinguish their own shepherd's voice even when other shepherds are speaking. In much the same way, Christians are—without being able to see God with clarity—supposed to be able to hear Him well. Receiving His Spirit enables us to tune in to God's "frequency" with increasing accuracy.

If we will practice doing it. Although we have been designed to hear God's voice, choice still seems to be involved. That's why Jesus implores, "Whoever has ears, let them hear" (Matt. 11:15). Earlier in the history of God's chosen people, the Lord pleads, "My people, hear my teaching; listen to the words of my mouth" (Ps. 78:1).

It's quite common for us to ignore His voice so often that we lose much of our ability to distinguish it. We are like teenagers who tune out our parents' voices when they ask us to do household chores. After a while, we genuinely do not hear what they are saying. We develop selective hearing, and their words do not register. We can do the same with God's voice, to the point that we might as well be deaf.

Other times, it isn't so much tuning Him out as it is not learning His "language." Really understanding what He is saying is as important as really hearing His voice in the first place. Jesus observed this phenomenon among the people around Him when He pointed out, "This is why I speak to them in parables: 'Though seeing, they do not see; though hearing, they do not hear or understand'" (Matt. 13:13). The prophet Jeremiah complained, "Which of them has stood in the council of the Lord to see or to hear his word? Who has listened and heard his word?" (Jer. 23:18).

The Holy Spirit can guide us into all truth, if we will let Him. He wants to do it. He will help us understand the message that has been "encrypted" in the words. With His help, and with the help of the Bible (see 2 Tim. 3:16) and gifted people (see Eph. 4:11-15), we can begin to understand more.

Often, a word from the Lord is not words at all, spoken or unspoken. God's language includes symbols and signs and physical manifestations. Hebrews 5:14 says, "But solid food is for the mature, who because of practice have their senses trained to discern good and evil" (NASB).

The Spirit uses "body language" all the time. Discerning the voice of God can come naturally as we come to understand that our bodies are a temple, and we were made to feel and discern the presence of God. For example, when my wife begins to feel tingling up and down her left leg, it is an indicator that the Holy Spirit is speaking to her to prophesy. This manifestation experience has happened at church, in restaurants, and on airplanes. We can feel these indicators from the Holy Spirit at any time or moment, but we must be aware enough to respond when they happen. For me, when I feel electricity and heat in my hands, I know that there is a healing angel being activated to heal those around me, as well as to impart healing anointing to those who want to go to greater levels of breakthrough in the healing ministry. Additionally, in my mind I continually hear God saying that He wants to heal, as He nudges me along in my thoughts and core beliefs.

Let's Talk About It

God's non-verbal communication can be very individual and personal. Talk about some of the special and specific ways God gets or directs your attention. What are the normal ways God speaks to you?

The better we know God, the more we understand what He is like. That helps us interpret our circumstances in the light of His character. Simply knowing what kind of a God He is can help us tell the difference between the truth and a lie.

For example, if a person who has cancer hears, "I [God] have given you this cancer to teach you a lesson [or to keep you humble]," you can know it's a lie. For one thing, God does not give people cancer. He is not the author of sickness. He is Yahweh Rapha, "the Lord, who heals you" (Exod. 15:26). Satan is the one who comes to steal, kill, and destroy, while Jesus always brings life (see John 10:10).

A woman who was dying from fourth-stage breast cancer came up to me during a healing conference in Detroit, Michigan. She explained that she could not be healed, because God had specifically told her that He had given her cancer to teach her humility so that she would rely on Him alone. She was convinced that she had heard God correctly. After all, the cancer had not gone away.

I told her that she had *not* heard God, who can only speak the truth, because those were lying words. Shocked, she assured me that God had spoken those very words, clearly. But as I began to explain what the true God is like, that He is always good and does good things, that He wanted to heal her and not kill her, she began to weep. Set free by the truth about God, she could then absorb His healing presence as I prayed for her.

She felt the change, and her doctor, who tested her and declared her cancer-free, confirmed it a few weeks later. I am sure that this woman got healed because she was able to hear the true message that Jesus was speaking to her. When we truly hear Him, His words will never return empty, but will accomplish what He desires and achieve the purpose for which He spoke them (see Isa. 55:11).

Jesus' life was not consumed with miracle services, crusades, and conferences. Rather, He simply lived His life displaying the nature of the Father everywhere He went. Jesus said things like, "When you have seen me, you have seen the Father" (see John 14:9) and "I and the Father are one" (John 10:30). People followed Him because they knew He was connected with the Life Source.

Jesus was only able to meet the needs of the people because He spent time with His Father and continued to always lean in to hear the voice of His Dad. From this place of confidence, He confronted every place of sickness, poverty, and darkness in the humanity around Him. He was not affected or swayed by the present earthly realm. He lived in the faith realm where anything is possible, making Heaven a present reality while He lived on earth.

He wants His treasure hunters to be able to do the same—and to go on to do even greater works than His when He walked on earth over 2,000 years ago (see John 14:12)!

Let's Receive It

I pray that you would be able to hear the living, breathing words of God as He communicates His plans and purposes to you. I release the grace to do what He speaks to you, so that His will can be done through your life. I release increased measures of faith as you become more and more confident that you are truly hearing Him.

Let's Do It!

1.) Try to get specific words of knowledge for each member of the group.

2.) Spend three minutes listening for God's voice. Share what you heard with the group.

3.) Put yourself in a place this coming week in which you will have to hear from God so that you can minister to someone. Then next week, share with your group how it went.

SEVEN

Be a Bigmouth: Preparing to Be a Prophetic Person Promotes Revival

You can't go treasure hunting without clues, and getting the clues depends on getting prophetic words and words of knowledge. Being able to share supernatural insights with people about what God thinks about them often proves to be the crucial key in opening their hearts to receive the Good News.

When we write down clues for our treasure maps such as "marriage problems," "hopelessness," "grief," or something obscure and unlikely, those clues provide a launching point for prophetic engagement once we have located the potential treasure. Such words of knowledge help us to find the "X" on the treasure map, and further prophetic insights help us dig deeply enough to unearth the treasure. Our "digging" is not premeditated, but instead emerges naturally in the course of a conversation with someone.

Hidden Clues

We ourselves may not be aware of the significance of our word choices. I learned this principle some time ago when I was praying for a man named Steve during a ministry time after a church service. He had not given me any details of what he wanted prayer for, except that he really needed to hear from God regarding a crucial decision that he needed to make.

I prayed for him as I normally did on such occasions, focusing on general prayers of comfort and encouragement, attempting to give him hope that God would speak to him regarding the situation and give him the specific strategies he needed to be able to work through the details. I went on to quote some Scriptures about God's faithfulness and His ability to provide for everything.

I finished praying, and Steve thanked me with no apparent evidence of anything significant having transpired. A few weeks later, however, he informed me that my *prophetic* prayer had provided the specific detailed answers for the decisions he needed to make that very day.

He told me that in the middle of my prayer, unbeknown to me, I had started addressing him as Stephen. He continued, saying that the Lord had audibly spoken to him a few times in the past, and that He had always addressed him as Stephen. He clarified that he had never referred to himself as Stephen, and that no one knew him by that name. So when I "accidentally" started calling him Stephen, it caught his attention. Then, without my being aware, the words of my prayer had prophesied the very solutions he needed, giving him the exact details he needed for the crucial decision he was under pressure to make.

Prior to this incident, I had never considered myself to be a prophetic person, even though when I felt an overwhelming unction on occasion, I could give someone a simple, general prophetic word with a certain amount of confidence. Candidly speaking, the prophetic people I had met were on the eccentric, sometimes bizarre side. I didn't consider myself one of them. I had never pursued prophetic ministry because I did not share those eccentricities. I did not think it was part of my calling and responsibility to demonstrate the Kingdom through prophetic words.

Yet here in this experience with Steve/Stephen, I learned that God can speak through me prophetically, even when I am not consciously aware that He's doing it. I began to learn, along with the rest of the people at Bethel Church, to carry the prophetic everywhere I go, looking for opportunities to use it. I learned that *speaking* God's will is just as important as *doing* God's will in bringing Heaven to earth. I became more willing to aspire to be a prophetic person, living a naturally supernatural lifestyle all day long.

Let's Talk About It

Share with each other how God has made you more open to and aware of prophetic senses and words of knowledge. How have you sometimes ignored His voice or even resisted it? How is He using this book and your group discussions to make you more eager to hear Him?

The Purpose of Prophecy

Paul taught that prophetic utterances are meant for "strengthening" or "edification" above all (see 1 Cor. 14:3). Interestingly, Paul does not list "judgment" as one of the uses of the prophetic ministry. This should eliminate from our minds the mental picture of the fiery, wild-haired prophet shrieking denouncements. Most prophetic people look and act just like you and me.

The way a person views God will determine the way he or she prophesies His will. If the person sees God as a condemning and judging Father, prophetic statements will tend to focus on sin and shortcomings. On the other hand, if the person prophesying knows that God always intends to lead us toward redemptive solutions, then his or her prophetic statements will reflect that.

It is not prophecy to simply announce a diagnosis. Just about anybody can state the obvious: You have a problem; you are in a crisis, in need of counseling, or bound in some way. But it is only through truly prophetic insights that God can express valid and timely answers to those personal problems. Hidden glory, missing identity, and unfulfilled destiny can only be called out prophetically. They are like pure gold. Thus, true prophecy is looking for gold—the good plans and purposes that God has for their lives. This is at the heart of a treasure hunt.

Throughout the Scriptures, God had His prophets proclaim the solution along with stating the obvious problem. He always highlighted the prophetic potential of His people and the redemptive purposes that He wanted to fulfill. The purpose of prophetic utterances is to expose a person to his or her true identity and destiny, to expand the person's view of life, and to show the person that God has something better in store for their lives.

Prophetic utterances do not have to be expressed in King James English, nor do they need to have "thus saith the Lord" appended to them. In fact, the best ones are expressed in plain English (or whatever language the person receiving the word speaks). Many times, the prophetic element simply infuses a normal conversational interchange.

Naturally, some people have trouble accepting that the hidden inspirations that inform the words of a prayer or a gesture of friendship are indeed prophetic. They have always viewed prophecy as something that seems otherworldly, and they expect it to involve fore-telling future events. They believe they can identify a true prophecy only when those events that have been foretold subsequently come to pass.

Foretelling future events is a valid form of prophecy, but it is not the only form. There are two kinds of prophecy: *foretelling* and *forthtelling,* or expressing the will of God for a person or a circumstance. A useful term for this is "calling out someone's destiny." We do this all the time in treasure hunting.

Finding and Mining the Gold

Sometimes the prophetic possibilities of an encounter are hard to spot. Many of the treasures in front of us do not look like treasure to our unseasoned eyes. But with prophetic help, we can find the gold in people, even when our initial focus may be only on the dirt.

Here's a good example of what I mean. I had been conducting healing meetings in Miami for four long days and I was exhausted as I waited to board my flight home. The flight was full and the ticket agent had not secured the aisle seat I had requested, which left me in the middle seat all the way back to California.

As I boarded and made my way down the aisle to my assigned seat, I was greeted by a screaming baby and her mother in the window seat next to mine. I tensed up as I realized the implications of the imminent altitude changes on this already unhappy baby. The baby was lying in its mother's lap with its head hanging over into my assigned seat. The aisle seat was empty, though, so I sat in it in faith, praying that the owner would not show up. All I wanted to do was sleep all the way home after the extended weekend of heavy ministry.

I stared toward the entrance of the plane, willing the person not to show. Just as I began to feel confident that nobody was coming to claim my seat, two gypsies came into view in the front of the plane. I held my breath. The taller of the two slid into a seat toward the front, and I let out a sigh. The shorter gypsy kept walking, however, and as I frantically scanned the remaining seats, I realized that I was sitting in the gypsy's seat.

The closer he came, the more obvious it was that this man had not bathed in a long time. He had dreadlocks down to the middle of his back, accented with a full beard that hung in clumps from his face. He was wearing an open-chested, puff-sleeved shirt with strands of demonic-looking necklaces hanging around his neck. His circus-style pants were tight around the ankles and ballooned out toward his waist. He wore hemp sandals and he was carrying a backpack and a small hand drum. He looked like Charles Manson meets Mr. Homeless meets Bob Marley, although he appeared more South American than Jamaican.

I looked back and forth between the crying baby and the Manson gypsy. He stopped at my seat. I did not even have to ask. I unbuckled the seat belt that I had previously put on by faith and moved over to my middle seat where I was sandwiched between a wild-eyed, screaming little head and satan personified.

Desperate, I made an internal declaration: This is it! I am not going to take any more of this. I am going to release the justice of God into the atmosphere. I am going to preach the Gospel to these people next to me all the way to California, whether they like it or not. If they don't, they can leave!

I turned to the woman next to me, introduced myself, and began prophesying over her baby. I started calling out his destiny, and then I proceeded to get a word of knowledge about a parent who was ill. She told me that she was on her way home from visiting her father who had just suffered a heart attack and was still in the hospital. I began to prophesy things about his life that convinced her that God was in this.

Within ten minutes, we were like long-time friends. Her baby even stopped crying, which was the greatest miracle of the day. I began to inquire about her husband, at which time she began to cry, telling me that he was unemployed and was very discouraged about getting a job in his field. I began to prophesy specific things about his heart's desires and God's purpose to help him, and her tears turned to relief.

We spent another ten minutes or so talking about God's plan for her life. She confessed that she was a Christian, but had not been going to church because of a recent move and her husband's depressed mood. When I asked if she would like me to pray with her, she readily agreed, and we prayed together for God's purposes to be fulfilled in her life and her family.

Let's Talk About It

In the story you have been reading, would you consider the prophetic element to be foretelling or forthtelling? Why? Would it have looked "religious" (with eyes closed or raised toward Heaven, etc.) or like an ordinary conversation? Can you picture yourself doing something like this?

Then I turned to the gypsy sitting in my coveted aisle seat. He was engrossed in the novel *The Da Vinci Code.* I opened the conversation with, "It's interesting that you are reading that book about the journey of a man trying to find the truth about Jesus because you're about to have an encounter in which Jesus reveals Himself to you." That got his attention. He put the book down to inquire how I had determined his fate.

I explained that God often gives me insights for people to show them how much He cares about them. He shrugged his shoulders, indicating that he wanted to return to the book. But I continued, "You're like Thomas in the Bible. God is going to show up when you least expect it." His expression turned to shock. He informed me that his name was Thomas, and that he had been on a one-year journey, traveling around the world searching for the true God.

He had never heard about the Thomas of the Bible, so I showed him the passage out of my Bible. His eyes grew bigger with each word. When he finished reading, he exclaimed, "That's me. This is crazy. How did you know my name was Thomas?" I explained that God knew his name and had just given me the idea of the story about Thomas. We spent the next four hours talking about his life and God's good purposes for him.

As it turned out, he was the son of a millionaire and was a world-class athlete who had, only two years prior, been a member of the Portuguese national rugby team. He said that he had left everything to find the truth about God.

When we finally landed and disembarked from the airplane, he introduced me to his traveling partner and we hugged like father and son. In the end, I did not get a wink of sleep on that flight, but instead encountered treasure that made for a trip of a lifetime.

Prophesy to the Bones

We have a responsibility to prophesy to the people we encounter, bringing Heaven to earth in a tangible way. We must exhale what we have inhaled from His presence. The world is waiting for us to breathe on them.

Ezekiel had a vision of what this looks like:

The hand of the Lord was on me, and he brought me out by the Spirit of the Lord and set me in the middle of a valley; it was full of bones. He led me back and forth among them, and I saw a great many bones on the floor of the valley, bones that were very dry. He asked me, "Son of man, can these bones live?"

I said, "Sovereign Lord, you alone know."

Then he said to me, "Prophesy to these bones and say to them, 'Dry bones, hear the word of the Lord! This is what the Sovereign Lord says to these bones: I will make breath enter you, and you will come to life. I will attach tendons to you and make flesh come upon you and cover you with skin; I will put breath in you, and you will come to life. Then you will know that I am the Lord.'"

So I prophesied as I was commanded. And as I was prophesying, there was a noise, a rattling sound, and the bones came together, bone to bone. I looked, and tendons and flesh appeared on them and skin covered them, but there was no breath in them.

Then he said to me, "Prophesy to the breath; prophesy, son of man, and say to it, 'This is what the Sovereign Lord says: Come, breath, from the four winds and breathe into these slain, that they may live.'" So I prophesied as he commanded me, and breath entered them; they came to life and stood up on their feet—a vast army (Ezekiel 37:1-10).

Notice that God did not breathe on the dead bones, although He could have done so, since He is the source of all life (see John 11:25). Rather, He commanded Ezekiel, the "son of man," to do it.

Likewise, our job is to prophesy—to be the conduit for the breath of God to flow into those who need supernatural life. It is similar to how the apostle Paul described our role in the world: "We are therefore Christ's ambassadors, as though God were making his appeal through us" (2 Cor. 5:20). On this earth, we are Jesus' hands and feet, as well as His mouth, and He wants to breathe into people; He wants to exhale!

When we prophesy, our words ride on the breath that is expelled from within us. Prophesying is simply exhaling in the Spirit, and the words that we speak, combined with the breath of the Spirit, bring life.

Let's Talk About It

Looking at the next section of text, "The Power of Our Words," as well as the previous one, discuss with each other on a personal, experiential basis what it means to prophetically "exhale" in the Spirit.

_____

_____

_____

_____

_____

_____

_____

_____

_____

_____

_____

_____

_____

_____

_____

_____

_____

_____

_____

_____

_____

_____

_____

_____

_____

_____

_____

_____

_____

_____

_____

The Power of Our Words

We have the opportunity to bring life through the prophetic words that we speak. Solomon pointed out, "The tongue has the power of life and death" (Prov. 18:21a). In other words, our prophetic words have the ability to release the supernatural power of God.

In Genesis 1, when God created the universe and everything in it, He spoke and it came into existence. His word—His speech—had innate power to perform His will. It is as though each word has a specific mission to carry out God's plans and purposes.

The prophet Isaiah wrote:

As the rain and the snow come down from heaven, and do not return to it without watering the earth and making it bud and flourish, so that it yields seed for the sower and bread for the eater, so is my word that goes out from my mouth: It will not return to me empty, but will accomplish what I desire and achieve the purpose for which I sent it (Isaiah 55:10-11).

So then, the words that we receive from the Lord carry the power to perform the purpose for which He has breathed on us. His name carries supernatural power, and when we receive and release His Word, supernatural empowerment and breakthrough become possible. I believe that this principle explains why the gift of the word of knowledge is so effective in releasing physical healing, which is why I try to remember to utilize it wherever I go.

Recently, I was visiting the construction site for a Bible college in India. Upon finishing the tour of the grounds, I expressed to our guide that I felt like God wanted to heal a tumor of someone on the construction site.

He began to make inquiries and soon found out that the caretaker's wife was suffering from advanced breast cancer and had a huge tumor. Once I communicated to her the word of knowledge that I had received, I prayed for her. Immediately the tumor dissolved, and all of the pain subsided. Along with her husband, she began to cry tears of joy. She was completely healed by the Word and the Wind, as I simply exhaled what I had inhaled.

When we release one of God's names (in this case, Healer), the Spirit will empower the words to accomplish His will. It just requires the faith to exhale what we receive from His breath—His presence.

Jesus said, "…What I have heard from him [the Father] I tell the world" (John 8:26). In other words, Jesus breathed out—He spoke what He had breathed in from the Father. John the Baptist confirmed that Jesus testified (spoke) about only what He had seen and heard. He added, in verse 34, "For the one whom God has sent speaks the words of God, for God gives the Spirit without limit" (John 3:34; see also John 3:32).

In the middle of a life-threatening storm, Jesus spoke to the wind and the waves and they become completely calm. The disciples were so amazed that they responded: "What kind of man is this? Even the winds and the waves obey him!" (Matt. 8:27). In the next chapter, Jesus spoke to a paralyzed man saying, "Get up, take your mat and go home" (Matt. 9:6), and the man was completely healed. Our words have power.

Some people brought a man who was deaf and mute to Jesus, begging Him to lay His hands on him so that he could be healed. Instead, after putting His finger in the man's ears and putting His spit on the man's tongue, Jesus spoke to the man, saying, "Be opened," and immediately his ears were opened, his tongue loosed, and he began to speak plainly—he was healed of every disability (see Mark 7:31-35).

Isn't it interesting that Jesus spoke to a man who could not hear? Why did He do that? Because He knew that there was power in the words He spoke, regardless of whether or not they could be heard by the ears of the deaf person. Jesus' words carried power because He spoke them from the Father's presence—He spoke out what He had breathed in.

Jesus spoke a word of forgiveness to a prostitute, and she was forgiven and set free (see John 8:3-11). He spoke to demons and they came out on command (see Matt. 8:16,32). The lame walked, the deaf heard, and the blind saw because He spoke the living, breathing Word of God wherever He went (see Matt. 4:23-24).

On one occasion, Jesus spoke to a fig tree, and it immediately withered (see Matt. 21:18-19). Obviously, Jesus has the power of life and death in His tongue. When His disciples wondered aloud at what had happened to the tree, Jesus told them that they could do more than wither a fig tree; they could speak to a mountain and it would be cast into the sea (see Matt. 21:21).

Jesus didn't move any mountains that we know of. But He said *our* words could do that! Like Jesus, we convey God's utterance—His speech—we communicate His creative will. Through the Holy Spirit's power, we can make a difference wherever we go.

How to Get Words of Knowledge

How do treasure hunters get such simple, accurate clues? They merely ask the Holy Spirit to give them these "words of knowledge" to provide them with clues for the divine appointments where the treasures are waiting.

A word of knowledge, or "message of knowledge" (1 Cor. 12:8) is simply knowing details about someone or something that you could not have known without the Holy Spirit telling you. Pay attention to what crosses your mind, because God plants words of knowledge in the form of thoughts. You may find it difficult to determine the significance of a thought. Words of knowledge do not come with pedigrees and instructions, most of the time. In fact, they often seem like random thoughts you could have come up with on your own. But if you're expecting God to speak to you this way, He can convince you of the validity of a thought and give you enough faith to step out and test it.

Most of the treasure-hunting stories in this book involve words of knowledge. When a word of knowledge is utilized in witnessing, it creates an undeniable invitation into a divine encounter, which often results in found treasure.

Jesus used words of knowledge all the time. Here's an example:

When Jesus saw Nathanael approaching, he said of him, "Here truly is an Israelite in whom there is no deceit."

"How do you know me?" Nathanael asked.

Jesus answered, "I saw you while you were still under the fig tree before Philip called you."

Then Nathanael declared, "Rabbi, you are the Son of God; you are the king of Israel" (John 1:47-49).

Nathanael was keenly aware that only God or someone who represented God could have known the specific details of his character and whereabouts. And it was that revelation that prompted him to declare, "Rabbi, you are the Son of God." Interestingly, that simple, yet specific and insightful word of knowledge led to Nathanael becoming one of the twelve disciples, and this happened even though he had originally been very skeptical when he said, "Nazareth! Can anything good come from there?" (John 1:46).

It only makes sense that if Jesus used this gift to find treasure, so should we. Sure, you can find treasure without inside information, but why aimlessly search and dig through the soil when the equivalent of a spiritual metal detector is available? The "word of knowledge" is an effective resource, accessible to every believer, to accomplish the task of finding the treasure and fulfilling the Great Commission.

According to First Corinthians 12, this gift, along with the others listed, "is given for the common good" (1 Cor. 12:7). In other words, having inside information about something or someone is supposed to be good for everyone. Sadly, some people occasionally use the gift to hurt other people by revealing their sins to everyone around. Jesus, however, demonstrated honor and respect when He used it, sharing the insight quietly with the person whom it concerned.

Jesus was not interested in exposing people, but rather in redeeming them. Most people already know what is wrong with them. What they do not know is what is *right* about them—what their destiny is in Christ and the good plans and purposes He has for them.

Let's Talk About It

What was the most recent word of knowledge you received? Was it obvious or subtle? How did you determine whether or not it had come from the Spirit? Who was it for? What did you end up doing with the word?

Words of Knowledge on the Radio

I was in Ecuador working with a network of churches to equip, empower, and activate them in a supernatural lifestyle. While in the city of Cuenca, I was invited to speak on a radio station with over 10,000 listeners. With translation, I began to speak about living a naturally supernatural life—sharing testimonies of how signs and wonders, miracles, healing, and the prophetic should be a natural part of the believer's life.

Ten minutes into the program, the phone lines began to light up as listeners heard about the hope of healing coming through the release of God's supernatural Kingdom. They were calling in desperation, wanting to get healed. The staff became frantic, trying to keep up with the volume of calls, and informed me that they had never before received so many calls during a show.

The first woman who called said that she had pain in her kidneys and feet. I could sense her desperation and immediately began to release the Kingdom of God to her over the airwaves. She expressed that she felt a fiery heat throughout her body and could feel healing coming into her feet and kidneys.

Without really thinking, I asked through the translator, "What about your head? Do you have a headache?"

"*Sí*," she responded in Spanish.

I continued, "Do you have pain in your neck and your shoulders?"

"*Sí!*" she exclaimed.

"How about your lower back?"

"*Sí!*"

"What about your knee?"

"*Sí!* How do you know all of that?" she inquired.

I explained that God showed me her pain because He wanted to heal every part of her.

I released the fire of God to her, and in about thirty seconds, she was completely healed from head to toe. She testified that all of the pain had left her body and that she was now standing on her feet, which was miraculous in itself because prior to the phone call she had been paralyzed!

Caller after caller shared their desperation for healing, and time after time God's power was released to make them well. The radio station had never had so many calls; a one-hour show turned into two! We could have kept going all day long. The phone lines were still lit up as we walked out the door to our next appointment!

God Uses a Mistaken Word of Knowledge

Also in Ecuador, our team of about thirty School of Supernatural Ministry students was invited to minister in the intensive care unit at a children's hospital. Upon arriving, we were informed that there were fifteen separate intensive care wards, with approximately thirty children in each ward. In order to minister to each critically ill child, we decided to separate into teams of three, including a translator.

As my team worked our way around the intensive care unit we were assigned to, many of the children there, and most of their parents, experienced amazing supernatural healing breakthroughs. Along with healing prayer, we then prophesied to each one about the good plans and purposes God had for them. Amazingly, several of them asked Jesus into their hearts, and others rededicated their lives to the Lord.

About forty-five minutes into this time, I felt that I had a word of knowledge for a nurse who had a hurt left foot. Taking the translator with me, I approached the nurses' station and asked if any of them had a hurt left foot. All eight of them looked at me with blank expressions, indicating that none of them had such a problem. I asked again, looking at each one of them as though they may not have heard me the first time. Each one shook her head *no.*

The collective group of nurses was now gazing at me as though they were deer in the headlights, "Are you sure none of you has a problem with your left foot? I really felt as if God wanted to heal someone's left foot." They assured me that they would surely know whether or not they had that problem, giving me a look that communicated, "Leave us alone."

So, I went back to the patients, and began ministering to one of the young girls and her parents. About five minutes later, as I was preparing the girl for healing, I could feel a presence behind me. I looked over my shoulder to find three nurses standing behind me with their arms crossed.

My initial thought was, *Oh great, these nurses think I am a kook, and they are going to ask me to leave the hospital.* I asked through the translator whether they could wait a few minutes while I finished helping this girl and her parents. They nodded, and I thought to myself, *Well, at least I'll get to minister to one more patient before being kicked out!*

A few minutes later, after ministering to the girl, I turned to the nurses, asking them how I could help them. The first nurse explained that while none of them had a hurt left foot, she did have a torn rotator cuff. She went on to explain that she had just seen the doctor overseeing the intensive care ward, and his advice was to have surgery; she would also be unable to work because of her inability to lift her patients.

The second nurse had just informed the first nurse that she had the flu and was going to have to go home, leaving the intensive care unit understaffed. I forget the third nurse's ailment, but all three were instantly healed and went straight back to work!

About five minutes later, the first nurse, who had just been healed, came back to ask if I would come to the nurses' station. When I arrived, there were a dozen or so nurses from nearby stations gathered around needing healing for various ailments. All of them were instantly healed, and before long, nurses from all over the hospital were lined up out the door because they had heard about their co-workers being healed.

The scene looked like a raucous New Year's Eve party, as the healed nurses expressed their excitement. Many of them received Jesus and were filled with the Holy Spirit, laughing uncontrollably.

One nurse, who had just been healed, stood against the wall, laughing and confessing that she felt like she was drunk. She later went home and convinced her son and his girlfriend to attend our evening meeting at the local church. They came, and both of them were healed. They asked Jesus into their hearts that night!

All of this came about over a wrong word of knowledge. God came anyway—because I stepped out and took a risk. In fact, He exploded onto the scene.

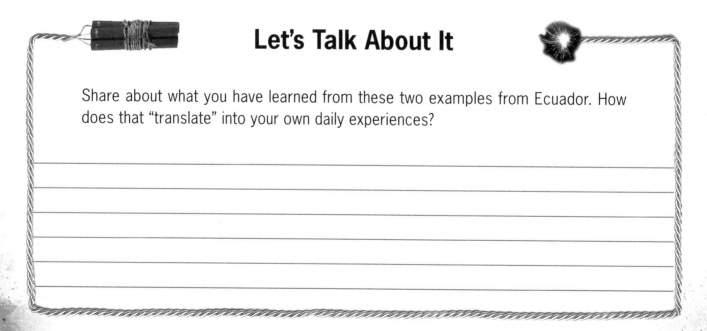

Let's Talk About It

Share about what you have learned from these two examples from Ecuador. How does that "translate" into your own daily experiences?

God invites us every day to step out and act on words and impressions that He gives us. Even as you consult the Lord for a sense of timing, the important thing is to act on what He gives you. Sometimes you will work prophetic senses and words of knowledge into a conversation with a stranger in a store or your neighbor in passing. Other times, you will be able to minister prophetically in a church setting. The reward for stepping out is to see people getting touched by the revelation that God cares about their daily lives.

New parts of your heart will come alive when you activate your faith in this way. God shows up and brings healing and redemption to people who need it. Best of all, it's fun!

 ## Let's Receive It

I release an increase in specific words of knowledge, and the ability to risk releasing them to those around you. I pray that you would have His heart when you prophesy to people, and that you would be a gold digger as you uncover people from the dirt they may be living in. May you be a mouthpiece of God to call forth the good plans and purposes that He has for everyone, so that each comes into his or her true destiny.

Let's Do It!

1.) Prophesy the good plans and purposes that God has for each person in the group. How do you feel afterward? Do you feel more inspired to devote yourself to God's plans and purposes? How does hearing God's word to you change the way you think, feel, and want to act? How do you think people who do not yet know God will respond when they hear this kind of prophetic approach?

2.) Give a prophetic word to someone you know this week. What was his or her response? How did it impact you?

3.) Give a prophetic word to a stranger this week. What was his or her response? How did it impact you?

EIGHT

What's the Catch?
Filling the Treasure Chest Is Fulfilling Revival

A graduate of our Bethel School of Supernatural Ministry was on her way to church one Sunday morning when she came upon an accident. She instantly knew that she was supposed to stop; she felt compelled to try to help in some way.

After parking on the side of the freeway, she noticed a man lying on a gurney. Oddly, no one was around him, so she went over to see if he might need prayer. As soon as he saw her, he exclaimed, "You're the angel. You're the angel."

"No, I'm not, but I am a Christian," she responded.

Once again, looking up at her, he countered, "No, you're the angel that I saw just before the accident!"

She countered once again, "Sir, I'm really not an angel, but could I pray for you?"

He agreed, telling her that as a result of the accident he could not feel his legs; he was paralyzed from the waist down.

Without hesitation, she began to release the Kingdom over him, and immediately he threw his legs over the side of the gurney and stood up. He began running around her and the gurney, shouting out that he was completely healed. On the spot, she led him into a relationship with Jesus.

Just then, a highway patrolman came over to where the two were rejoicing and demanded to know what was happening. He was very upset because he had left the man in a paralyzed condition just a few minutes earlier. The student looked at the officer and simply said, "Well, Jesus just healed him, and Jesus just saved him."

The officer shot back, "That's ridiculous!" Turning toward the man, he asked him what had happened to enable him to walk.

He said, "Like she said, officer, Jesus just healed me, and Jesus just saved me!"

Now perturbed, the patrolman said, "I can't write that on the report."

The student countered, "Then we can't sign it."

Resigned, the patrolman began to write, mouthing the words as he wrote: "Jesus healed him, and Jesus saved him."

When we find that we are filled with sudden compassion, as this student was, we should recognize God's fingerprints on an encounter. We will be more motivated to stop, and we will find that we really do have the ability to meet the needs of those we reach out to. It is a partnership to release the Kingdom—doing God's will on earth as it is in Heaven.

God's part is to provide the supernatural motivation, and our part is to have the willingness to reach out. It was only after Jesus was filled with compassion that He followed with the statement, "I am willing" (Mark 1:41). After that, Jesus touched the man who had leprosy, and as a result, the man was immediately cured (see Mark 1:42). When we are willing to take the risk of touching those around us who have intimidating needs, we can release supernatural possibilities. When we touch people as a result of being motivated by compassion, supernatural power is activated.

Treasure, Treasure Everywhere

Everywhere you go, you cross paths with people who desperately need a real encounter with God. They are in stores, businesses, neighborhoods, parks, schools, and even in the church. When God uses someone like you or me to find them and to meet their overwhelming needs and the unfulfilled desires of their hearts, they are eternally grateful.

God is grateful, too. Jesus told a parable that captures God's heart for lost treasure. It goes like this:

Suppose a woman has ten silver coins and loses one. Doesn't she light a lamp, sweep the house and search carefully until she finds it? And when she finds it, she calls her friends and neighbors together and says, "Rejoice with me; I have found my lost coin." In the same way, I tell you, there is rejoicing in the presence of the angels of God over one sinner who repents (Luke 15:8-10).

We as Christians too often see the "lost coins" in the world as worthless, instead of viewing them as the treasure depicted in the parable. It can be so very easy to think of a sinner as a lost cause, and therefore not even worth seeking. It is true that many of them are "darkened in their understanding and separated from the life of God because of the ignorance that is in them due to the hardening of their hearts" (Eph. 4:18), but that should not deter us from uncovering the treasure within them. Everyone is worth finding.

 ## Let's Talk About It

How can you differentiate between the supernatural compassion God gives you and the ordinary level of compassion that comes from your human nature? How can you develop your ability to respond more quickly when God wants to send you into a situation? Talk about the times when you may have failed to respond to God's "nudges"—as well as the times when you have aligned yourself with His will, presumably with good results.

How He Found Me

I am grateful that my grandmother and cousin did not see me as a lost cause before I became a Christian as a sixteen-year-old. My grandfather, who had been a deacon in the Baptist church, had just passed away, so my cousin had gone to take care of my grandmother in Southern California. I decided to spend my vacation with them that summer, mostly so

I could spend time at the beach and enjoy unlimited partying. What I did not realize was that, thanks to Grandma's influence, my cousin had become a Christian.

I was fully into all that the world had to offer a teenager at the time. A drug-using, rock-and-roll drummer, I was so far away from Christ that I was the last person any of my friends would think could become a Christian. I would come home from the beach, eat every available food item in the house, and constantly mock the Christian television shows that Grandma and my cousin watched throughout the evening.

What made it possible for me to change? It was my grandmother's unconditional acceptance of me, even with all of my sinful baggage, and my cousin's convincing argument that I could go to church with them "as is." That church happened to be Calvary Chapel in Costa Mesa, California, and the time happened to be 1975, at the height of the Jesus Movement.

I showed up for a Saturday night concert high on drugs and expecting to hear organ music and see "dorks" in short-sleeved white shirts with ties. What I found, however, was 2,000 people who were just like me on the outside, but on the inside they had found something that I had not even been looking for. That night, I found out what it was.

No one judged me; I did not need to be judged because I already knew what was wrong with me. What I did not know was what was right with me or that God had a plan for me. Every lyric of every song seemed to have been written especially for me; they expressed my heart's desire for intimacy and significance.

As the preacher got up to give the altar call, I sat there contemplating the choice I was about to make. I knew that following Christ meant giving up all of my sinful practices, which were like crutches that had not really helped me anyway. I knew I would have to give up my "friends," even though I often felt agonizing loneliness in their company. I also knew I needed help for my frequent suicidal thoughts that were brought on by the gnawing emptiness I felt every day.

But I just could not take the leap. I was afraid of the unknown and of the false perception I had of the Church and Christianity. I sat there through two altar calls in which a couple of hundred "wannabe" treasures went forward to be discovered. The preacher began to pray for those who had come forward as I sat lower in my seat next to my cousin, who was fervently praying for me under his breath.

Then the minister stopped. He apologized for stopping at such a crucial moment, but he felt that there was just one more person who needed to respond to God's love that night. Briefly, he mentioned that God had a special plan for this person's life, and that if he or she would just come forward, that person's life would never be the same because God's love and freedom would satisfy every need and desire.

Instantly, my heart began to race at 8,000 RPMs. I knew he was talking to me. I had never felt so much love and sense of purpose. I felt an invisible hand pick me up by the back of the collar of my T-shirt, and the next thing I knew I was running to the front of the church, accompanied by the exuberant applause of 2,000 amazed believers! That night, I was the ultimate treasure.

Before I was a Christian, I appeared to be an unlikely "coin" to have had that much effort employed to find me. In my mind, I was worth about as much as a scuffed-up old penny that someone would gladly throw into a wishing well, aware that the gesture was in vain, but relieved to be rid of the little nuisance in his pocket. It felt strange to me that God not only knew me, but also cared enough about finding me that He would have a preacher stop in the middle of his prayer to highlight me out of all those people.

That night, I felt like treasure. I realized that God does not make junk. I was like the lost coin in the parable. I was so valuable to God that He put all of His focus on finding me. He orchestrated search teams like my grandmother and cousin, who relentlessly wooed me out of my dark hole. Looking back, I know there were many others who had gone out of their way to shine a searchlight in my direction and point the way to the truth. I do not know any of their names, nor would I likely recognize any of them if I met them face to face today. But one day, when we all meet in Heaven to revel in the great treasure hunting adventures that we pursued in this world, I have a feeling that there will be a crowd of those who contributed to the treasure hunt to find me.

No other place in Scripture depicts all of the angels "rejoicing" except in the parable of the lost coin. I guess if all of Heaven is that excited over a treasure hunt, it must be a pretty important event in the Kingdom of God. Jesus paid a great price, spending Himself on purchasing these coins. Therefore, just as you would spare no resource searching for a "collectable," so you should also go to all lengths to locate one lost person. And our Father in Heaven will celebrate that person's return, just as the father who found his son in Luke 15:24 proclaimed, "He was lost and is found."

Let's Talk About It

Consider your own conversion story in light of the story about the lost coin. What can you share about it with the others in your group? How were you lost? How were you found? How have you recognized that you were and are a "treasure" to God?

Making Disciples, Not Just Converts

The final objective of the treasure hunt is to get the treasure into the treasure chest; it is to get the convert into the Church. In the parable of the lost coin, the implication is that God is not content to leave the coin where He had found it, but instead He called all of His friends together to rejoice with Him in what He had found. The treasure hunt, then, is not over until the lost coin is safely stored with the other coins in the treasure chest.

Another way of stating this is that the goal of the treasure hunt is to make disciples of those we find with our clues. Jesus' Great Commission to us was to make *disciples*, not only converts. Here is what He said:

Jesus came to them and said, "All authority in heaven and on earth has been given to me. Therefore go and make disciples of all nations, baptizing them in the name of the Father and of the Son and of the Holy Spirit, and teaching them to obey everything I have commanded you. And surely I am with you always, to the very end of the age" (Matthew 28:18-20).

At Bethel Church, we love to see people encounter Christ out in the community, but we really get excited when we hear that they have been connected to a local church, whether it is ours or another church in the city. We are interested in the expansion of the Kingdom, not necessarily just the growth of our particular church. We realize that many people decide to go forward in a high-powered service to repeat a prayer, but making a decision to follow Jesus does not necessarily make a person a disciple. So when we see people get saved through our various outreach ministries, and then make their way into any church where they can get discipled, we rejoice all the more.

We do run into some Christians, however, who argue that a lack of follow-up is reason enough to discount the whole witnessing process. They contend that it does more harm than good to witness if you do not have the proper mechanisms for getting people into the Church. They use the same argument that I just used, namely that Jesus commanded us to make disciples, not converts.

To that I would simply say that before we can disciple them, we must first convert them through a born-again encounter. We must not allow ourselves to devalue witnessing just because the Church has done a poor job in making disciples.

In the early church, we are told "the Lord added to their number daily those who were being saved" (Acts 2:47). Just as it was the purpose of their witness, the purpose of our witness is to get people through the door of salvation and into the Kingdom, which the Church represents here on earth. Most of the time, getting someone into the Church is the best way to get that person into the Kingdom for keeps.

An Open Invitation to All

For a number of reasons, we do not always have the opportunity to bring someone to church. Still, we consider it a primary objective for our treasure hunters. With this in mind, we recommend that treasure hunters bring along a business-type card that shows church service times, contact information, and directions on the back. It can also be helpful, when possible, to get contact information from the "treasure" for further follow-up.

In the parable of the wedding banquet in Matthew 22, the directive was to invite *everyone* to the banquet. Although all the people in the vicinity were eventually invited, not everyone took advantage of the open invitation. People made all kinds of excuses, even though God's intention was to fill the wedding hall with guests.

The treasure hunt is like going to the "street corners" (the community) and gathering all of the people (treasures) we can find (see Matt. 22:8-10). It is important to remember, however, that our commission is only to invite them, not to force them to come. Notice that God's focus was on finding the people who would respond, not on those who did not. God was willing to get a lot of "No" responses in order to get some "Yes" ones. Now as then, His heart is to invite everyone in hopes that even a few will make their way into the treasure chest.

Although we do not successfully get everyone we meet into the treasure chest, our goal is to give him or her more than a one-time encounter. We must always keep in mind that supernatural encounters are signs that lead people into an ongoing relationship with God and connection with the family of God, the Church, where they can be nurtured into maturity and given the tools and support to live successfully in the Kingdom.

I have developed a twelve-week course called Firestarters that is designed to equip, empower, and activate new believers in a supernatural lifestyle of pursuing passion, purpose, and power. Since 2008, we have seen over 900 people go through our course at Bethel Church in Redding, California. It is amazing to see brand-new believers walking in their God-given destiny as revivalists, as well as being discipled in the faith. There is nothing like seeing the treasures shined up and ready for display!

Treasure Hunt Plus

I was on a treasure hunt recently in which people who were clearly on our treasure maps were refusing us. We were finally led to a man who had lost both parents to illness several years prior and then lost his lucrative job of many years. Subsequently, his wife had divorced him, after which he lost his home. He finally ended up on the streets as an alcoholic, which is where we encountered him.

He was no longer drinking, because he had gone through a program that had helped him get sober, but he still had no vision for his life. Consequently, he continued roaming aimlessly from town to town, taking odd jobs, just trying to find a break somewhere. The man was "clean-cut" and obviously sober, but he was visibly depressed over his unfortunate circumstances.

Interestingly, we were the last of three other teams that had been led to this same man. Without realizing it, all three teams had gone to work independently to try to find this man a place to stay where he could discover and begin to live out his God-given destiny. Giving the man directions, each of the teams had invited him to the local Firestorm meeting that evening. The man showed up, and when I asked if anyone wanted to know the good, kind God that we had been presenting and demonstrating through healing and prophetic words, this man was the first one standing. He invited Jesus into his life on the spot.

As it turned out later, one of the treasure hunt teams members arranged for the man to live at his house while he got discipled and sorted out his career options. Now he had an opportunity to enter into the plans and purposes that God had prepared for him. The treasure had come into the treasure chest!

Let's Talk About It

Discuss and share your personal orientation about evangelism. Have you tended to put more emphasis on being born again or on discipleship? Have you tended to discount one or the other as a result?

No Strings Attached

Jesus preached the Gospel wherever He went, healing the sick and setting people free, yet only four of those people were found at the cross with Him when He was crucified. Out of the more than 500 who saw Him after the resurrection (see 1 Cor. 15:6), only 120 were found in the Upper Room on the Day of Pentecost (see Acts 1:15). The point is that Jesus gave everyone a chance to get in, even if they did not take advantage of the opportunity. Nowhere do we ever see Jesus heal someone or set someone free with the pre-condition that he or she follow Him as a disciple.

On the contrary, sometimes He seems to make it difficult for people to follow Him. In the Gospel of Luke, we find a story of a demon-possessed man from the region of the Gerasenes (see Luke 8:26-39). This man had been harassed by a "legion" of demons, causing him to run around naked, homeless, and chained hand and foot. Once Jesus set him free, it seemed only natural for him to want to leave that place of torment in order to follow His Savior. Yet, even though the man pleaded with Him, Jesus sent him away and told him to go home instead and to testify about what had happened to him (see Luke 8:39).

Remarkably, when Jesus returned some time later (see verse 40), a crowd welcomed Him, even though not so long before all of the people of that region had asked Him to leave. And even though this formerly demon-possessed man had not been discipled, he had been able to continue in the revelation he had received, and he had influenced the entire region through his testimony.

Uncovering Treasures Through Encounters

I believe that many Christians shy away from witnessing because the only models they have seen are either very invasive or argumentative. How many of us enjoy being accosted with the salesman's pitch to get us to buy something we do not need or want? Often, Christians are perceived with the same unfortunate disdain as the unwanted salesman. How many of us cringe when we have to listen to the futile, fruitless arguments that occur in the lunchroom in the name of "witnessing"? As a result of unpleasant experiences, many of us decide to leave witnessing to others, not wanting to leave a bad taste in the mouths of non-Christians, and feeling that we need to protect the reputation of Christians and the Church.

This is not what the apostle Peter wanted people to do when he wrote: "Always be prepared to give an answer to everyone who asks you to give the reason for the hope that you have. But do this with gentleness and respect" (1 Pet. 3:15). He wanted us to "be prepared in season and out of season; [to] correct, rebuke and encourage—with great patience and careful instruction," as his fellow apostle Paul wrote in Second Timothy 4:2.

Some read these passages and assume that Peter and Paul are speaking about being prepared to present intellectual reasons for the hope that we have, or theological dissertations to prove the existence of God to even the most hardened atheists. I don't know about you, but I have rarely led someone to Christ through argument. Not because I cannot argue, but because at some point the debate requires a leap of faith. "It is by grace you are saved, through faith," not debate (see Eph. 2:8). A debate may be able to lead people to the point of deciding to take the leap, but it cannot force them to decide.

Billy Graham is a classic example of someone who is masterful at walking a crowd through the logical steps toward the launching pad of faith. But most people do not come into the Kingdom through a well-developed argument. They come through an encounter, whether it is a personal testimony of how someone else encountered God in some way, or a supernatural encounter in which God revealed Himself to them in a specific way.

A man with an experience is never at the mercy of a man with an argument. And a man with an argument is only one encounter away from changing his argument! At one time, Saul of Tarsus had developed a pretty good argument to the effect that Christians deserved to be persecuted to the fullest extent of the law. He spent all of his time, resources, and effort toward that end. Yet as soon as Jesus appeared to him personally on the road to Damascus, he was ready to change his argument. When Ananias showed up at the door a few days later by divine appointment, Saul gladly accepted the counter message of the Good News. Saul became Paul and he spent the rest of his life promoting the Gospel wherever he went.

Treasure hunting gives people an opportunity to experience the love and power of God firsthand. This is the most persuasive form of evangelism I know about.

"Drive-by" Healing and Conversion

My son, Chad, was part of a small ministry team that our church sent to the Houston Astrodome right after the devastation of Hurricane Katrina. They were able to pray for many people who desperately needed physical healing.

On one occasion, Chad was praying for a woman on a cot. As he was releasing God's presence to her, a man who was walking by shouted out, "What the h*** did you just do to me?" Chad looked up toward the startled man and assured him that he had not done anything. The man shot back, "Yes, you did! As I was walking past you, my knee felt like it was on fire! What did you do?" Chad explained that he was just praying for the woman on the cot.

After further inquiry, the man explained that he had had a knee injury that had debilitated him for years. As he was limping past Chad, God's fire had hit his knee, and he was now completely healed. Chad explained that the power of God must have spilled out onto the man as Chad was praying for the woman on the cot. The man received Jesus on the spot and left very happy!

Let's Talk About It

Discuss the phrase, "A man with an experience is never at the mercy of a man with an argument." See if you can cite some personal examples to support your observations.

_____

_____

_____

_____

_____

_____

_____

_____

_____

_____

_____

_____

_____

_____

_____

_____

_____

_____

_____

_____

_____

_____

Hunger Prepares the Way for Breakthrough

Apart from completely unexpected encounters such as the one in the Astrodome, spiritual hunger may be the most significant key to releasing the Kingdom in and through our lives. In Hebrews 11:6, we are promised that God "rewards those who earnestly seek him."

One of the nuanced meanings of the phrase "earnestly seek" in the Greek is to "crave." Accordingly, when we crave His presence and the resources of His Kingdom, He rewards us with His presence and power. Therefore, if we desire greater miraculous breakthroughs, we must make our continual goal to stay hungry. Hunger unlocks the resources of Heaven and releases them on earth.

David testified that "those who seek the Lord lack no good thing" (Ps. 34:10b). In Psalm 107:9, he further promises that "he [God] satisfies the thirsty and fills the hungry with good things." This was not only David's personal experience with God, but it is also a prophetic promise about the Messiah coming to bring the Good News (the good things) of the Kingdom.

In Luke 1:53, Mary sings these prophetic words, written by David, in response to the angel's announcement that she has been chosen to be the bearer of the Messiah: "He has filled the hungry with good things…." Could it be that the primary reason Mary was chosen to carry the Messiah in her womb was because of her hunger for God's Kingdom?

Could it be that the hunger of a few simple people like Simeon, Anna, and Mary attracted Heaven to earth? Could it be that "at just the right time" (Rom. 5:6) is determined by our hunger for God and His Kingdom? There was a 400-year season of silence prior to Jesus' coming. Could it be that hunger broke the silence and released the Good News?

In another example, Mary was the one who unlocked Heaven at the wedding at Cana when she asked her Son Jesus to provide wine for the wedding party (see John 2:1-11). Before she did that, Jesus had no intention of revealing His miracle-working power just yet. Mary was relentless in her request, even when Jesus chided, "Woman, why do you involve me?…My hour has not yet come" (John 2:4). Mary demonstrated her hunger for Heaven by turning a "deaf ear" to Jesus' response and commanding the servants, "Do whatever he tells you" (John 2:5). Water was turned into wine that day, which means that Jesus exposed Himself as the promised Messiah before the time that God had planned in Heaven—all because of Mary's desire to see God's intervention in a crisis.

In First Corinthians 14:1, the apostle Paul encouraged everyone to "eagerly desire spiritual gifts" (NIV 1984). Well before Paul's time, David testified in Psalm 21:2a, "You have granted him [the king] his heart's desire." In the same way, when you and I crave God's presence, we will be rewarded in turn with all of the good things of His Kingdom. Our hunger releases them.

It is the Father's heart to give us every perfect gift (see James 1:17), whether it is provision, encouragement, comfort, wisdom, signs and wonders, miracles, or healing. It is our hunger that attracts the good things that we want from God and His Kingdom.

I have found many times that, at the end of a meeting, someone will approach me who desperately needs a miracle. Even though I am completely exhausted, I will stop to pray for the person because of his or her hunger. In fact, the more hunger I sense, the longer I will contend with the person for a breakthrough miracle. I believe God responds to us in a similar fashion. When He sees our hunger, He shows up.

On the other hand, when I sense that someone is not really very hungry for me to pray for him or her, but instead conveys sort of a nonchalant attitude, I am not highly motivated to sacrifice and contend for a breakthrough with that person, and it is largely because I know already that not very much can happen when hunger is not present.

In Matthew 15:29-38, we read about the time when Jesus had been ministering to a multitude of people for an extended period of time. The disciples suggested that He send them away because they were hungry and there was not enough food to go around. Instead of sending them away, however, Jesus fed them. Just as Jesus did not turn away from hungry people when He walked the earth, so He does not turn away from those who hunger for His Kingdom now. God Himself is always motivated by the hunger and thirst of the people He loves.

In John 6:35, Jesus proclaimed, "I am the bread of life. He who comes to me will never go hungry, and he who believes in me will never be thirsty" (NIV 1984). Notice He does not say that we will not get hungry again, but rather that we will not continue to be hungry. In other words, our hunger and thirst will be satisfied, repeatedly, and that's why we will never experience lack.

 # Let's Talk About It

Can you identify a particular "Kingdom hunger" in yourself right now? How has Jesus most recently satisfied such a hunger for you? Thinking back to your own conversion or some other significant juncture in your Christian life, how do you think your hunger played an important part in the outcome?

Treasure Hunting Is a Lifestyle, Not an Event

God has called each one of us to partner with Him in releasing the Kingdom to those around us in whatever sphere of influence we find ourselves. Not only are we to partner in healing, but also in releasing all of the resources of the Kingdom, whether it is the prophetic, forgiveness, wisdom, revelation, comfort, service, or another aspect of Kingdom life. God's invitation into partnership with Him is not just a hopeful request. It is the responsibility of every believer. As Christians, it is up to us to unlock Heaven in order to provide Kingdom breakthrough for those who need God's intervention.

I was shopping at the local mall with my daughter one early evening when we came across Jerry, one of our School of Supernatural Ministry students. He had a slightly frantic look on his face as he informed us that he only needed "one more" before he could go home. Thinking he was after merchandise of some kind, we offered to help. He pulled out a piece of paper and asked if we had seen anyone with a wrist brace.

He went on to explain that he had been working on his treasure-hunting skills and had decided to train at the mall. He had written down ten words of knowledge and had vowed not to go home to his wife and four children until he had found all ten clues! Jerry is an amazing treasure hunter who has learned that treasure hunting is supposed to be a continual lifestyle rather than a one-time, programmed event.

I have received many reports from churches and individuals who are doing treasure hunts as a supernatural lifestyle. Some are meeting once a week to do group treasure hunts, while others are sitting for a few minutes each day to prepare a treasure map to take with them to work or to school. I even heard of one woman who does a treasure hunt each week with her sister who lives 3,000 miles away. They call each other to exchange clues, and then spend a few hours looking for them. Once they are done, they call each other to report what they found.

Each time I take teams from Bethel's School of Supernatural Ministry to do Supernatural Lifestyle conferences, I utilize the treasure hunt to equip, empower, and activate the churches we are working with into supernatural evangelism through supernatural encounters. Our hope, of course, is that they will gain confidence to continue to do supernatural evangelism once we are gone, whether it is utilizing the treasure hunt or some other creative strategy.

The treasure hunt is undoubtedly an effective mechanism to mobilize people for supernatural evangelism, but a person does not need to do a treasure hunt to do supernatural evangelism. It should be obvious by now that any believer, apart from doing a treasure hunt, can heal the sick, raise the dead, set people free, and lead people to Christ.

The point is to demonstrate the Kingdom through our witness in whatever creative ways God directs us, living naturally supernatural lives so that we exude His presence wherever we go. Treasure hunting is just one way of facilitating and promoting our ability to tap into the supernatural resources of the Kingdom to bring Heaven to earth.

And while the treasure map has proven to help us find treasures we would not have ordinarily considered, we do not necessarily need supernatural clues to find hidden treasure. There are treasures all around us, and we can find them as we inconvenience ourselves to stop for them. When our eyes are opened to the hundreds we pass by every day, we cannot help but be filled with compassion to offer the help that only God can supernaturally provide.

Jesus Wants to Get Out of the Box

If you are a believer, Christ lives in you. It is also true that the Christ who lives within you wants to live through you. Jesus wants to get out of the box; He wants to reveal His glory through ordinary (yet extraordinary) people like you and me. In fact, you may be the only representation ("re-presentation") of Jesus that some people will ever see. You may be their only hope for encountering God's glory.

To this end, the Bible is clear when it says, "We are therefore Christ's ambassadors, as though God were making his appeal through us" (2 Cor. 5:20a).

Isaiah commanded us:

Arise, shine, for your light has come, and the glory of the Lord rises upon you. See, darkness covers the earth and thick darkness is over the peoples, but the Lord rises upon you and his glory appears over you (Isaiah 60:1-2).

We are to reflect to the world the glory that is shining on us from God's presence. We are to reveal God's extraordinary goodness, as demonstrated in signs and wonders, miracles, healings, prophetic encouraging words, smiles, forgiveness, and practical acts of service to those around us. It is the kindness of God that leads to repentance (see Rom. 2:4). His kindness, reflected in His glory (released through us), attracts people to the good, kind, loving God whom they see being demonstrated in an extraordinary way.

This same command was reiterated by Jesus when He pointed out:

You are the light of the world. A town built on a hill cannot be hidden. Neither do people light a lamp and put it under a bowl. Instead they put it on its stand, and it gives light to everyone in the house. In the same way, let your light shine before others, that they may see your good deeds and glorify your Father in heaven (Matthew 5:14-16).

In other words, Jesus wants to shine through our lives; He wants to be let out of the box. Jesus Christ who lives within us has all of the answers that those around us are waiting for. Through Christ, we have access to every resource in Heaven in order to meet every need represented here on earth.

The treasure is out there, right now. What are you waiting for?

Let's Receive It!

I release you into your destiny as a world changer and a history maker. I pray that you will find favor and influence wherever you go and with whomever you meet. I declare that your family members, friends, neighbors, co-workers, and community encounter the goodness and kindness of God as you take risk to release His presence in power and proclamation of the Good News of great joy. I release new levels of breakthrough as you pursue a supernatural lifestyle. I declare that you are a treasure hunter, and God is going to use you to fill His treasure chest.

Let's Do It!

Go on a treasure hunt if you have not already done so. If possible, go out with the same group of people with whom you have just finished reading and discussing this book. Afterward, evaluate your experience. How can you incorporate the treasure-hunting model as a significant part of your lifestyle?

RESOURCE I

Creating and Using the Treasure Map

Over time, I have settled on the following method of conducting a treasure hunt. It seems to yield the best results, while always allowing room for the Holy Spirit to change the direction of the treasure hunt.

STEP ONE: On a pre-printed sheet of paper, each person writes down six words of knowledge in the spaces allotted for each of the following five categories (you should have a total of thirty clues when you are finished):

Location [e.g.: stop sign, bench, digital clock, coffee shop, Target, WalMart, etc.]

_____   _____   _____   _____   _____   _____

A person's name [usually first name]

_____   _____   _____   _____   _____   _____

A person's appearance [e.g.: color of specific articles of clothing, color of hair, glasses, etc.]

_____ _____ _____ _____ _____ _____ _____

What the person might need prayer for [e.g.: knee brace, cane, kidneys, tumor, left ankle, marriage, etc.]

_____ _____ _____ _____ _____ _____ _____

The unusual [lollipop, windmill, lime-green door, dolphins, etc.]

_____ _____ _____ _____ _____ _____ _____

STEP TWO: Form groups of three or four treasure hunters (no more than five).

Combine the words of knowledge of the group to make your treasure map. Do not combine them on a separate sheet; each person keeps his or her own list.

STEP THREE: Choose a beginning location.

Compare your other clues while you are on the way to your first location.

STEP FOUR: Start looking for the treasure.

STEP FIVE: When you find someone using one of the clues from the individual maps in the group…

- Approach the person in a friendly manner.

- Say something like, "This may seem a little odd, but we're on a treasure hunt and we think you're on our list."

- Show the person your list or lists; the clue may be one or two things from each list, or just one thing from one list.

- Build rapport. Make friends. Ask questions to get to know the person.

- Let the person know that God has highlighted him or her, and that God wants to bless the person.

- Pay attention to things that you can help the person with, and ask if you can pray for something.

STEP SIX: If the person says "no"…

- Build more rapport (common ground, friendship).

- Ask the Holy Spirit what He wants to highlight about the person.

- Give the person some encouraging prophetic words. (Avoid being "religious.")

STEP SEVEN: Ask the person again if you can pray for something.

If the person says "no" again, bless him or her and proceed to the next treasure (person).

If the person says "yes" (especially for healing prayer):

- Ask for the presence of God to come. (Release His presence on the person.)

- Command the pain to leave, bones to be set, back to be realigned, tumor to shrink, etc.

- Ask the person to test it out: "Do something that you couldn't do before we prayed."

- Repeat if necessary.

STEP EIGHT: After the person gets healed, or after you have blessed the person through prophetic words…

- Explain what just happened (the kindness of God revealed…He knows you and cares about you…).

- Ask the person if he or she would like to know Jesus personally (have a relationship with Him).

- If "yes," help the person to ask Jesus into his or her life.

- Provide any further follow-up that seems appropriate.

STEP NINE: Go to the next divine appointment on the treasure map!

The Use of the Treasure Map

1. Fold your sheet of paper in half from top to bottom so that your five sets of clues are facing you.

2. Fold the paper again from side to side so that half of your clues are on one side of the fold while the other half are on the other side. This makes the map less conspicuous, while still allowing you to view all of your clues by simply turning

your hand over. This may sound a little silly or overboard, but I have found that being as discreet as possible is more effective than drawing a lot of attention to the treasure hunting group, especially in a store or business.

3. Make sure that each treasure hunter in the group keeps his or her map available and accessible to each of the other team members. Many clues will be found by looking on another team member's map.

4. Do not put the map into your pocket, backpack, or purse. You know the saying, "Out of sight, out of mind." Most people who do not end up finding treasure are the ones who do not use their maps consistently.

5. The treasure map is like a puzzle; it requires concentration and creativity to put it together.

6. You can approach someone who matches only one clue on your treasure map. Often, you will find that he or she matches other clues once you begin to build rapport and ask penetrating questions.

7. Use your creativity and imagination. For example, "post office" could mean a mailbox, a mail delivery person, a mail store, the post office, or even a letter that someone is about to mail. A person's name could be the person you have approached, or it could indicate a friend, relative, or acquaintance of that person who needs prayer or reconciliation, or who has some other point of significance.

8. When you approach people, be sure to show them the clue on your map that led you to them. Remember, for most people, "Seeing is believing."

9. Approach people in twos or threes at the most. A large group can be intimidating. It is also less threatening for the person you are approaching if the group is mixed in gender. I usually prefer to limit a treasure-hunting group to no more than five, because that's the maximum number of people who can fit in the average vehicle. To form the groups, I will often select two of one gender and three of the other.

10. Do not split up your group of five for more than one encounter. Work as a team and continually touch base, checking your clues and changing around which team members are approaching potential treasures.

11. Children are great to have on treasure hunts. They are less threatening and often much better at the out-of-the-box creativity that can help with finding clues.

12. You might consider printing the instructions for conducting a divine encounter (Treasure Hunt Resource II) on the reverse side of the sheet of paper that's used as a map. Have each person on the team read these instructions before launching out.

13. After a successful divine encounter, find time to jot down the key parts of the testimony on a blank portion of the map. Share these later for mutual encouragement. If you collected contact information for this purpose, follow up with the person with whom you talked.

—Treasure Hunt—

RESOURCE II

How to Conduct a Divine Encounter (A Model for Healing Ministry)

Getting Started

1. Ask the person to tell you briefly what's wrong or what he or she would like prayer for.

2. If appropriate, ask the person if it would be all right for you to place your hand on the area that needs healing. (This is optional; it's not always applicable.)

3. Invite God's presence. Ask His Kingdom to come.

4. Listen for the promptings of the Holy Spirit to pray in certain ways or to follow certain strategies. Remain consciously willing to take risk.

5. Keep your eyes open while you pray. Watch for visible signs of God's action in or on the person.

6. Ask the person, "Are you feeling anything? Any sensations in your body such as heat, cold, peace, electricity…?"

7. Ask the person to check it out, to move or do something that was impossible or too painful before. Another way of asking would be to say, "Try to cause the pain you experienced before. See if it's gone."

8. If the person is now healed, rejoice together and give praise to God. Encourage the person to obtain a doctor's report for a physical healing.

If no breakthrough in healing…

1. Thank God for anything that is going on. (Thankfulness often releases breakthrough.)

2. Pray for increase. Then thank Him for the increase of His presence and healing.

3. Declare scriptural healing promises over the person, or share testimonies about other healings.

If pain gets worse or moves as you're praying…

1. Consider the possibility of a spirit of affliction or infirmity.

2. Take authority over such a spirit. (You do not need to yell, let them cough or vomit, etc.)

3. Release more of God's healing presence.

If no breakthrough or if pain increases…

1. Ask the person if there may be someone he or she needs to forgive.

2. If yes, ask the person to declare forgiveness out loud.

3. If no, simply pray again and release more of God's presence on the person.

4. Begin to prophesy hope and destiny over the person. (Some people do not feel worthy to be healed.)

5. Ask the person to check it out again, to do something that was impossible or too painful before.

If still no breakthrough…

1. Always encourage the person that God is good and is in a good mood.

2. Always encourage the person to continue to pursue breakthrough. Tell the person that sometimes God's healing touch comes later, after the prayer. Tell the person that when we pray, God's Kingdom comes, and when His Kingdom comes, good things do happen.

3. Encourage the person to give thanks for what did happen (what the person has been able to see or feel), even if there seems to have been only a small measure of breakthrough.

4. Always bless the person.

5. Never lay the responsibility on the person, even if the person has been resistant to healing or has little or no faith.

6. Let the Holy Spirit do His work.

RESOURCE III

STUDY GUIDE RESOURCES
Questions, Prayers of Impartation, and Treasure Hunt Activities

WEEK ONE
The Treasure Hunt:
The Making of a Modern-Day Revivalist

Let's Talk About It

Have you ever seen someone reach out to others in this way? What is your initial reaction to hearing about this kind of bold public witness? Are you intrigued? Nervous? Mystified? Cautious? (Give each other permission to be honest in your sharing.) Share an instance in which you have stepped across the chicken line in a public setting. Was it a positive or negative experience? Explain.

Let's Talk About It

Talk with each other about what it means to live a naturally supernatural life. Speak from your own experience as much as possible. How many ways can you encourage each other to press into God for more?

Share an encounter in which God gave you some inside information about someone. What was the response? How did you feel afterwards?

Let's Talk About It

Have you ever taken part in a treasure hunt or anything like it? If so, what was your experience like? Were you a treasure hunter—or were you perhaps the treasure? What did you learn (both helpful and corrective), not only about reaching out to strangers but also about yourself and about God?

Let's Talk About It

Discuss the motive of service (having a mindset of "what can I do for you?") as opposed to other motives for sharing the Good News. What are some other typical motives for undertaking one-on-one evangelism? What have you experienced in this regard? How do you think the particular methods of treasure hunting can help keep people focused on loving and serving others?

Let's Receive It

I release you into your true destiny as a world changer and history maker, along with the confidence that you have what it takes to represent God and His supernatural Kingdom in whatever sphere of influence He has placed you. I declare surprising, supernatural encounters during your quiet times, and daily activities in which God speaks to you and shows you specific ways to connect with the people He puts in your path. I pray that my ceiling would be your floor, and that you would begin to have your own testimonies of God's supernatural work through you!

Let's Do It!

1.) Fill out a treasure map. It should take about five minutes to get thirty clues. If it takes longer, you are probably working too hard. Remember, you have the mind of Christ, so your thoughts are the promptings of the Holy Spirit—write them down!

Then go on a treasure hunt with your group. You may want to do it as you go to lunch or coffee after your meeting. Select one person who seems to have the most confidence to lead out. Remember, when you find your treasure, make sure each person shows the treasure the clues they have on their treasure maps. Don't just tell them you have the clues; they must see them to believe them.

Go through the steps for a divine encounter with the treasure

Go to the next treasure

Afterward, debrief. How did the encounters go? How do you feel about taking a risk?

2.) Step out on your own one time during the next week to give someone a word of encouragement or to ask someone if you can pray for healing. Write down what happened and how you felt as you took a risk. Be prepared to share your experiences with the group when you meet next week.

WEEK TWO
Courage to Cross the Chicken Line:
Revival Risk Renders Radical Revivalists

Let's Talk About It

Where treasure hunting is concerned, where is your current "chicken line"? What can you do to cross it?

Let's Talk About It

Consider others types of risk beyond faith-risk, such as in my example of learning to ski, and talk about how you have grown as a result of taking increasingly challenging risks. Give some examples from your own life about taking various risks.

Let's Talk About It

Celebrate the recent risk-taking experiences of your group members and each other's incremental progress as risk takers, whether or not they resulted in notable breakthroughs. Encourage each other in particular for seeming failures.

Let's Talk About It

As a group, discuss your own experiences of "pushing the envelope" where risk is concerned. Has it caused you to grow in faith? What has stifled your risk taking? What may be holding you back right now?

Let's Talk About It

What risks did you take yesterday and today? Talk about why they were risks for you, even if others might not consider them to be risks. How did God come through for you? How can you be more intentional about stepping out in risk?

Let's Receive It

I release you into the next levels of risk—so that you would be able to cross the chicken line, leading to new adventures and breakthrough in bringing Heaven to earth on behalf of others. I pray that you would have complete confidence that when you take risk, God will come, and that when He comes, He will do good things because He is a good God in a good mood.

Let's Do It!

1.) Give each member of the group a word of encouragement. Try to get words of knowledge about each member of the group.

2.) Determine your next level of risk and make an action plan to do it by the next meeting. (Write down how it went—How did you feel? What was the outcome?—and so forth.) Be prepared to share your risk adventure with the group at the beginning of your next meeting.

WEEK THREE
Empowered by Joy:
Learning to Laugh Launches a Lifestyle of Revival

Let's Talk About It

Do you feel that you or anybody you know carries a full measure of God's joy—or at least a growing measure of joy? What would that look like, practically, in your life? How would people know that you had a full measure?

Let's Talk About It

What role has joy played in your Christian experience? How have you used joy and laughter as a resource of strength and empowerment in releasing the Kingdom of God to others?

Let's Talk About It

What is your experience of Spirit-impelled laughter? Why is it hard to separate "holy laughter" from natural laughter? Do we always need to distinguish between those two kinds of laughter? Why or why not?

Let's Talk About It

Does it surprise you that so many Scriptures speak directly about joy? Why do you think this subject has been so overlooked in the teaching of the Church? Can you think of other topics that were overlooked throughout Church history? How do you think we can restore the power of joy back to the Church?

Let's Receive It

I pray that you would encounter the laughter of Heaven in your everyday life. I release the grace to use your fruit of self-control to choose laughter by faith, even when you don't feel like it. May you be able to see and hear His laughter over you as you encounter His good mood toward you. As you align yourself more and more with the joy of the Lord, may you find the supernatural empowerment you need to release His presence and power to those around you who need to encounter His good mood.

Let's Do It!

1.) Practice laughing with your group. (It may feel awkward and strange at first.) Don't stop! Try to go at least ten minutes. How do you feel? Was or is it hard for you to feel comfortable laughing? Explain.

2.) Purpose to laugh as you go through your week. Share your journey of joy with the group next week.

WEEK FOUR
You Have What It Takes! Fostering Relationship with the Father Fuels the Fire of Revival

Let's Talk About It

When you stop and think about it, have you also assumed that Jesus must have somehow silently consulted the Father every single time He did something? What difference does it make in your daily life to realize that He didn't—and that His heavenly power and will to love others everywhere is always resident in you?

Let's Talk About It

Talk about your experience of relating to God as *my* Father instead of *the* Father. Why do you think it is so important to know God as *our* Father, *my* Father?

Let's Talk About It

Do you believe—really believe and act on—the fact that you can bring Heaven to earth? Is your belief in the theoretical realm, or have you proved it? If you have proved it by your actions, what did you do and what was the result?

Let's Talk About It

Which member of the Trinity do you tend to address most often in your prayers? Talk about possible reasons for your answer. Over the years, how have your prayers changed as your relationship with God deepened? What evidence can you share regarding your growing awareness of your sonship or daughterhood?

Let's Talk About It

Why can we say that God's anointing is for everybody, regardless of his or her personalities, gifts, and personal history? Talk about times you have stopped short of operating in the anointing, settling instead for the limits of your own strength. How can you muster the courage to take new risks of faith?

Let's Receive It

I release an encounter in which you hear your heavenly Father say, "You are My daughter/son." I see new levels of confidence in declaring, "Your Kingdom come, Your will be done." I declare that you have what it takes to be a treasure hunter that changes the world wherever you are.

Let's Do It!

1.) Begin to declare God's will over specific things in your life that need His intervention. Release His presence and power through the words you proclaim.

2.) Utilize your status of sonship or daughterhood throughout the week. Journal the breakthroughs you get, and report back to the group next week.

WEEK FIVE
The Naturally Supernatural Lifestyle:
Relaxing Releases More Revival

Let's Talk About It

See if each of you can come up with a true story of a time when relaxing your effort was the best way to success. It doesn't have to be a prayer story to illustrate the principle. After you have come up with some illustrations, see if you can put the principle into words.

Let's Talk About It

Practically speaking, how can you relax in overwhelming circumstances and needs in order to better release the Kingdom? Share with each other what you have learned about this principle.

Let's Talk About It

What do you think working out of rest looks like? Share an example from your own life about how you accomplished more with less effort. What prevents you from resting? What are some ways in which you can sustain a lifestyle of rest?

Let's Talk About It

Create some "what if" scenarios, either using scriptural accounts or modern-day testimonies of how miracles were instrumental in convincing people of the truth of Christ. What if no healing or miracle had occurred? Would unbelievers have been convinced that a loving God is alive and worth turning to? On the other hand, what if an unmistakable supernatural component had been introduced into a situation? What might have transpired? Why is supernatural healing so important in communicating the Good News?

Let's Talk About It

Talk about an experience, firsthand or otherwise, in which God's supernatural power came into a situation without apparent effort on anybody's part. What did you learn from the experience? How did you make use of what you learned?

Let's Talk About It

Have you sometimes neutralized your prayers by failing to pray out of full confidence that God would come and act (essentially saying, "may Your Kingdom come—please, if it be Your will")? Talk about how you can develop the habit of *declaring* the coming of the Kingdom of God. How can you be sure that your declarations match up with God's will?

Let's Receive It

I release a new level of revival rest over you and into you. I pray that you would hear the words that Jesus heard at His baptism, "With him I am well pleased"–that you would have complete confidence of His approval of you before you ever even attempt to take risk to release God's Kingdom. I pray that your vision will expand to better see those who are waiting for an encounter with God. I release you into a new level of risk in declaring God's purposes in seemingly insurmountable circumstances.

Let's Do It!

1.) Take some risk this week to release God's Kingdom to someone, and then share a testimony with the group about it. How did you reach out to someone this week who needed an encounter with God? How was he or she able to encounter "our Father"?

2.) Write down the instances in which you found yourself working for approval from God and man this week. How were you able to revert to revival rest? Or not?

WEEK SIX
Hanging on to Every Word:
Hungering for the *Rhema* Releases Revival

Let's Talk About It

How do you most often hear God? What part do the Scriptures play in it? Tell the others in the group about a time when God spoke to you in a new-to-you way and how you recognized that it was Him.

Let's Talk About It

Talk about times when you doubted that you were hearing God's voice. What made you waver? In the end, what helped you discern?

Let's Talk About It

How do you make yourself more open to hearing God? How do you stay hungry? Share a time in which you heard God say to do something out of your comfort zone and you obeyed.

Let's Talk About It

How do you and God communicate? What do you do if the communication you are hearing is contradictory to the Scriptures? How do the Scriptures work together with visions, dreams, ideas and thoughts, and prophecies? Can God say things and give us ideas that are not found in the Scriptures? Why or why not?

Let's Talk About It

God's non-verbal communication can be very individual and personal. Talk about some of the special and specific ways God gets or directs your attention. What are the normal ways God speaks to you?

Let's Receive It

I pray that you would be able to hear the living, breathing words of God as He communicates His plans and purposes to you. I release the grace to do what He speaks to you, so that His will can be done through your life. I release increased measures of faith as you become more and more confident that you are truly hearing Him.

Let's Do It!

1.) Try to get specific words of knowledge for each member of the group.

2.) Spend three minutes listening for God's voice. Share what you heard with the group.

3.) Put yourself in a place this coming week in which you will have to hear from God so that you can minister to someone. Then next week, share with your group how it went.

WEEK SEVEN
Be a Bigmouth: Preparing to Be a Prophetic Person Promotes Revival

Let's Talk About It

Share with each other how God has made you more open to and aware of prophetic senses and words of knowledge. How have you sometimes ignored His voice or even resisted it? How is He using this book and your group discussions to make you more eager to hear Him?

Let's Talk About It

In the story you have been reading, would you consider the prophetic element to be foretelling or forthtelling? Why? Would it have looked "religious" (with eyes closed or raised toward Heaven, etc.) or like an ordinary conversation? Can you picture yourself doing something like this?

Let's Talk About It

Looking at the next section of text, "The Power of Our Words," as well as the previous one, discuss with each other on a personal, experiential basis what it means to prophetically "exhale" in the Spirit.

Let's Talk About It

What was the most recent word of knowledge you received? Was it obvious or subtle? How did you determine whether or not it had come from the Spirit? Who was it for? What did you end up doing with the word?

Let's Talk About It

Share about what you have learned from these two examples from Ecuador. How does that "translate" into your own daily experiences?

Let's Receive It

I release an increase in specific words of knowledge, and the ability to risk releasing them to those around you. I pray that you would have His heart when you prophesy to people, and that you would be a gold digger as you uncover people from the dirt they may be living in. May you be a mouthpiece of God to call forth the good plans and purposes that He has for everyone, so that each comes into his or her true destiny.

Let's Do It!

1.) Prophesy the good plans and purposes that God has for each person in the group. How do you feel afterward? Do you feel more inspired to devote yourself to God's plans and purposes? How does hearing God's word to you change the way you think, feel, and want to act? How do you think people who do not yet know God will respond when they hear this kind of prophetic approach?

2.) Give a prophetic word to someone you know this week. What was his or her response? How did it impact you?

3.) Give a prophetic word to a stranger this week. What was his or her response? How did it impact you?

WEEK EIGHT
What's the Catch? Filling the Treasure Chest Is Fulfilling Revival

Let's Talk About It

How can you differentiate between the supernatural compassion God gives you and the ordinary level of compassion that comes from your human nature? How can you develop your ability to respond more quickly when God wants to send you into a situation? Talk about the times when you may have failed to respond to God's "nudges"—as well as the times when you have aligned yourself with His will, presumably with good results.

Let's Talk About It

Consider your own conversion story in light of the story about the lost coin. What can you share about it with the others in your group? How were you lost? How were you found? How have you recognized that you were and are a "treasure" to God?

Let's Talk About It

Discuss and share your personal orientation about evangelism. Have you tended to put more emphasis on being born again or on discipleship? Have you tended to discount one or the other as a result?

Let's Talk About It

Discuss the phrase, "A man with an experience is never at the mercy of a man with an argument." See if you can cite some personal examples to support your observations.

Let's Talk About It

Can you identify a particular "Kingdom hunger" in yourself right now? How has Jesus most recently satisfied such a hunger for you? Thinking back to your own conversion or some other significant juncture in your Christian life, how do you think your hunger played an important part in the outcome?

Let's Receive It

I release you into your destiny as a world changer and a history maker. I pray that you will find favor and influence wherever you go and with whomever you meet. I declare that your family members, friends, neighbors, co-workers, and community encounter the goodness and kindness of God as you take risk to release His presence in power and proclamation of the Good News of great joy. I release new levels of breakthrough as you pursue a supernatural lifestyle. I declare that you are a treasure hunter, and that God is going to use you to fill His treasure chest.

Let's Do It!

Go on a treasure hunt if you have not already done so. If possible, go out with the same group of people with whom you have just finished reading and discussing this book. Afterward, evaluate your experience. How can you incorporate the treasure-hunting model as a significant part of your lifestyle?

About Kevin Dedmon

Kevin Dedmon has a traveling ministry focused on equipping, empowering, and activating the Church for supernatural evangelism through signs and wonders, healing, and the prophetic. He earned a Master's degree in church leadership from Vanguard University, and has been in full-time ministry for more than 25 years. He and his wife are part of Bethel Church staff in Redding, California.

www.kevindedmon.com

In the right hands, This Book will Change Lives!

Most of the people who need this message will not be looking for this book. To change their lives, you need to put a copy of this book in their hands.

> *But others (seeds) fell into good ground, and brought forth fruit, some a hundred-fold, some sixty-fold, some thirty-fold* (Matthew 13:8).

Our ministry is constantly seeking methods to find the good ground, the people who need this anointed message to change their lives. Will you help us reach these people?

> *Remember this—a farmer who plants only a few seeds will get a small crop. But the one who plants generously will get a generous crop* (2 Corinthians 9:6).

EXTEND THIS MINISTRY BY SOWING
3 BOOKS, 5 BOOKS, 10 BOOKS, OR MORE TODAY,
AND BECOME A LIFE CHANGER!

Thank you,

Don Nori Sr., Founder
Destiny Image
Since 1982

DESTINY IMAGE PUBLISHERS, INC.

"Promoting Inspired Lives."

VISIT OUR NEW SITE HOME AT
WWW.DESTINYIMAGE.COM

FREE SUBSCRIPTION TO DI NEWSLETTER

Receive free unpublished articles by top DI authors, exclusive
discounts, and free downloads from our best and newest books.
Visit www.destinyimage.com to subscribe.

Write to: Destiny Image
              P.O. Box 310
              Shippensburg, PA 17257-0310

Call: 1-800-722-6774

Email: orders@destinyimage.com

For a complete list of our titles or to place an order
online, visit www.destinyimage.com.